DAY BY DAY
WITH ST. FRANCIS

"Make me a channel of your peace."

DAY BY DAY
WITH
ST. FRANCIS

MINUTE MEDITATIONS FOR EVERY DAY
CONTAINING A QUOTE, A REFLECTION,
AND A SCRIPTURAL PRAYER

By
Peter A. Giersch

Illustrated

CATHOLIC BOOK PUBLISHING CORP.
New Jersey

CONTENTS

NIHIL OBSTAT: Rev. Daniel P. O'Mullane, S.T.L.
Censor Librorum

IMPRIMATUR: ✠ Most Rev. Arthur J. Serratelli, S.T.D., S.S.L., D.D.
Bishop of Paterson
August 28, 2015

Scripture quotations (unless otherwise noted) are taken from the ST. JOSEPH NEW CATHOLIC BIBLE® Copyright © 2019 by Catholic Book Publishing Corp. Used with permission. All rights reserved.

(T-179)

ISBN 978-1-941243-31-2
© 2015 Catholic Book Publishing Corp., N.J.
Printed in China   21 HA 3
catholicbookpublishing.com

INTRODUCTION

WHEN Jorge Mario Bergoglio stepped onto St. Peter's balcony on March 13, 2013 to become the first Jesuit Pope in the history of the Catholic Church, he also became the first Pope to take the name of Francis. This may not have been so remarkable if he had chosen the name in honor of the famous Jesuit missionary, St. Francis Xavier, but in fact, he chose the name to call to mind the founder of the Franciscans, St. Francis of Assisi, immediately signaling to the world to get ready for the unexpected.

There have been four Franciscan friars who have become Popes. While none of these four Franciscan Popes is remembered as the embodiment of the Franciscan style, it hasn't taken long for Pope Francis to remind the world of the charism of St. Francis. Whether it's paying his own hotel bill, refusing to live in the Papal apartments or owning—and driving—a used car, Pope Francis has definitely channeled the kind of attitude that most people would think of when they think of St. Francis of Assisi.

But Pope Francis is human, and the papacy can be a long and complicated journey. There's no telling how this will play out over time. St. Francis himself was a human being whose life was almost certainly more complicated than we can imagine. What is really at the heart of the word Franciscan is not any man, not even Francis himself, it is the action of the Holy Spirit. While the virtues and attributes we call Franciscan go by many names—the spirit of St. Francis, the Franciscan Tradition, the Franciscan Way, etc., what we are referring to here is the action of the Holy Spirit inspiring virtue in the Christian faithful.

Each religious order, whether it be Franciscan, Jesuit, Carmelite, Dominican, has been a channel for the Holy Spirit to reveal to the Church a particular way of living as a Christian. The unique virtues embodied in each order is referred to as their charism—a Greek word meaning "gift."

So while this book is about St. Francis, his life and writings, it is really about the Holy Spirit, and particular gifts given to the Church that we refer to as Franciscan. In these pages we will share in the manifold ways in which the Holy Spirit works in and through the Christian Church in that special way we refer to as "Franciscan."

As with all prayer books, this book will yield the most fruit when accompanied by a little solitude and silence. In the spirit of the ancient Christian method for Bible reading, it is not necessary to try to grasp the entire passage in one sitting. Rather, just look for a word or a phrase or a simple concept that jumps out at you. Sometimes it is even just a single word that strikes you. Take that away with you and ruminate on that for the day.

One of the unique things about Francis and the writings associated with this great Saint is the liberal use of Scripture and the striking way in which Francis' life was such a perfect living out of the words of Christ. In fact, in his encyclical on the life of St. Francis, Pope Pius XI went so far as to say that, "there has never been anyone in whom the image of Jesus Christ and the evangelical manner of life shone forth more lifelike and strikingly than in St. Francis." Perhaps for this reason, it seemed appropriate to give, after each day's reflection, a Bible verse for the prayer starter. In itself, each Bible verse can serve as an aid to prayer, but for those who want to go deeper into each day's reflection, the Bible verse may lead you to pick up your Bible as a way to appreciate more fully the evangelical counsels and scriptural principles that make up the way that we call "Franciscan."

Writings of St. Francis are few and there is much scholarly debate over which of the documents attributed to him are authentically works of his hand. A devotional book such as this does not enter into those debates. Suffice it to say that our aim was to use for our reflection documents that are widely agreed to be authentic in their representation of the Franciscan charism.

You will find here all the works that are confirmed by scholars to be genuinely authored by Francis. These works are framed for context by *The Life of St. Francis* of St. Bonaventure, from

Salter's English translation of 1904. Bonaventure's *Life of Francis* is the only biography authorized by the Franciscan Order and a powerful devotional in its own right.

Our book ends with passages from the Papal Bull *Mira Circa Nos* in which Pope Gregory the IX proclaimed Francis' canonization. Also included for reflection here is the famous "Prayer of St. Francis" in a new translation by the author. The prayer was almost certainly not written by Francis, but has come to be accepted as representative of the Franciscan charism.

The Bible verses are taken from the New Catholic Version.

HE grace of God our Savior has appeared in His servant Francis unto all who are taught by his example to utterly deny ungodliness and worldly lusts and to live after the manner of Christ.

JAN. 1

Bonaventure, *The Life of St. Francis*, Prologue, 1

REFLECTION. Thus begins St. Bonaventure in his prologue to *The Life of St. Francis*. In the words, "to live after the manner of Christ" he perfectly summarizes the example of Francis.

Our path toward holiness will involve stripping ourselves of anything that prevents us from growing more like Christ.

PRAYER. *It is now no longer I who live, but it is Christ who lives in me.* (Gal 2:20)

HUS He gave him for a light unto believers, that by bearing witness of the light he might prepare for the Lord the way of light and peace in the hearts of the faithful.

JAN. 2

Bonaventure, *The Life of St. Francis*, Prologue, 1

REFLECTION. As with any of the Saints, Francis is God's gift to the faithful, to inspire them to holiness.

Thus each Christian lives as an ambassador for Christ and the Gospel, giving witness to the world.

PRAYER. *We are ambassadors for Christ, since God is appealing to you through us.* (2 Cor 5:20)

HAT the true story of his life might be handed down the more assuredly and clearly, I went to the place of his birth, and held diligent converse with his familiar friends that were yet living.

Bonaventure, *The Life of St. Francis*, Prologue, 2

REFLECTION. St. Bonaventure echoes the introduction to the Gospel of Luke and the Acts of the Apostles.

The Christian record of God's action in the world is not the stuff of legend, but rather the simple record of eyewitnesses.

PRAYER. *I, too, after researching all the evidence anew with great care, have decided to write an orderly account for you.* (Lk 1:3)

 HERE was a man in the city of Assisi, Francis, whose memory is blessed, for God delivered him in His mercy from the perils of this present life, and abundantly filled him with the gifts of heavenly grace.

JAN.
4

Bonaventure, *The Life of St. Francis*, 1, 1

REFLECTION. Francis was delivered from the dangers of this present life by God's grace.

All of us must be similarly delivered. We cannot achieve godliness and holiness on our own.

PRAYER. *Apart from me you can do nothing.*

(Jn 15:5)

FRANCIS was both drawn away by his Father's calling, and weighed down toward earthly things, and had not yet learned to contemplate heavenly things, nor accustomed himself to taste of the divine.

JAN. 5

Bonaventure, *The Life of St. Francis*, 1, 2

REFLECTION. It is easy to forget that so many of the Saints were just average human persons, like ourselves, until they were changed by God's grace.

This transformation is something we all long for and pray for.

PRAYER. *Proclaim the praise of him who has called you out of darkness into his marvelous light.* (1 Pet 2:9)

THE hand of the Lord was upon him afflicting his body with protracted sickness, so that He might prepare his soul for the anointing of the Holy Spirit.

JAN. 6

Bonaventure, *The Life of St. Francis*, 1, 2

REFLECTION. It cannot be denied that God uses suffering to prepare us to receive the gifts of the Spirit.

The time of suffering and temptation that Jesus knew in the desert is played out in each of our lives.

PRAYER. *Jesus was led by the Spirit into the desert to be tempted by the devil.* (Mt 4:1)

FRANCIS said: "Lord, what will Thou have me to do?" And the Lord said: "The vision that thou has seen shall be spiritually wrought, and is to be fulfilled in thee not by mortal counsel, but by divine." **JAN. 7**

Bonaventure, *The Life of St. Francis*, 1, 3

REFLECTION. Francis at first understood God's call to worldly success in battle, but did not know that God's call was spiritual.

How often does some prompting of the Holy Spirit lead us to expect a worldly result, when in fact the real action of God is within us.

PRAYER. *"Not by strength, nor by might, but by my spirit," says the Lord.* (Zec 4:6)

HE WITHDREW him from the stir of public business, devoutly praying. And it was whispered unto his spirit that the warfare of Christ is to be begun by victory over self. **JAN. 8**

Bonaventure, *The Life of St. Francis*, 1, 4

REFLECTION. The Saint reaches the knowledge that must accompany any successful endeavor: we must first learn to control ourselves and win that battle before we win any other.

Time alone with God quickly reveals that the biggest battle is inside of us.

PRAYER. *A person without self-control is like a defenseless city.* (Prov 25:28)

HE WOULD seek lonely places and there he devoted himself without ceasing to groaning and won an answer from the Lord. "If thou will come after Me, deny thyself, and take up thy cross, and follow Me."

Bonaventure, *The Life of St. Francis*, 1, 5

REFLECTION. The battle for self-mastery is won by self-denial.

And this is why holiness is such a challenge, it requires denying our own ego.

PRAYER. *What is the source of your fighting and bickering? It is the selfishness at war within you!*

(Jas 4:1)

HE PUT on the spirit of poverty, the feeling of humility, and the love of inward godliness.

Bonaventure, *The Life of St. Francis*, 1, 6

REFLECTION. Francis began by renouncing all things, all honors, and all outward things that separated him from God.

This simple formula that Francis found for gaining mastery over the self is simply to combat the universal desire to possess, consume, and control.

PRAYER. *All these things come from the world: the lust of the eyes, the lust of the flesh and the pride of life.*

(1 Jn 2:16)

13

PROSTRATING himself before an Image of the Crucified, he heard with his bodily ears a Voice proceeding from the Cross, saying: "Francis, go and repair My House which is falling utterly into ruin." **JAN. 11**

Bonaventure, *The Life of St. Francis*, 2, 1

REFLECTION. The Church of God is the Body of Christ, and every gift of the Holy Spirit is given for the building up of that Body.

It would take Francis some time to understand that "My House" referred not to the physical Church but to Christ's Body on earth.

PRAYER. *Christ is the head of the body, which is the Church.* (Col 1:18)

BUT when his father learned that the servant of God was tarrying with a priest, he dragged him into the house and afflicted him with words, stripes, and bonds. But Francis was the more eager to carry out that which he had begun. **JAN. 12**

Bonaventure, *The Life of St. Francis*, 2, 2

REFLECTION. Like many who strive for holiness, Francis did not have the full support of his family. In fact, like Aquinas, his family tried to physically stop him from serving God.

This is a great trial that requires a true infilling of the Holy Spirit to endure.

PRAYER. *Whoever comes to me and does not hate his father and mother . . . and even his own life, he cannot be my disciple.* (Lk 14:26)

14

OMING to the Bishop, he at once took off all his garments, ... and stood up naked, saying to his father: "Hitherto I have called thee my father, but now I can confidently say 'Our Father, Which art in heaven.'"

JAN. **13**

Bonaventure, *The Life of St. Francis, 2, 4*

REFLECTION. This famous scene from the life of Francis is a powerful example of what it takes to leave everything to serve God.

In perhaps less dramatic fashion, we are all called to renounce everything and stand naked before God.

PRAYER. *Let us lay aside all the sin and anything which weighs us down, distracts and clings to us.* (Heb 12:1)

HEREAFTER, this despiser of the world, left the city, and, glad and free, sought hidden solitude where he might hearken in loneliness unto the treasures of the divine converse.

JAN. **14**

Bonaventure, *The Life of St. Francis, 2, 5*

REFLECTION. The long tradition of holy men and women seeking solitude and silence is well attested and true.

How might we, in our daily lives, "leave the city" to find hidden solitiude for the treasure of divine discourse?

PRAYER. *When you pray, go to your room, close your door, and pray to your Father in secret.* (Mt 6:6)

THEN that lover of humility took himself to the lepers, . . . serving them for the love of God. Lo, as the servant of the lepers, Francis, touched that loathsome sore with his holy lips, the disease utterly vanished.

JAN.
15

Bonaventure, *The Life of St. Francis*, 2, 6

REFLECTION. As we approach the first miracle of Francis we see how his radical pursuit of holiness led to a radical act of God.

Francis lived the Gospel fully, in all ways.

PRAYER. *The one who believes in me will also do the works that I do, and indeed will do even greater ones.* (Jn 14:12)

FRANCIS, now established in the humility of Christ, recalled the obedience laid upon him by the Crucifix as to the repairing of the church of San Damiano, and like one truly obedient, returned to Assisi.

JAN.
16

Bonaventure, *The Life of St. Francis*, 2, 7

REFLECTION. Perhaps nothing distinguishes the servant of God quite as much as the ability to hear and obey.

To hear and obey fellow humans is hard enough, but the Saint rightly hears and promptly obeys God's subtle urgings.

PRAYER. *If you will indeed obey my voice then you shall be a special treasure to me above all people.* (Ex 19:5)

AYING aside all shame, he went about begging from those who had known him in his affluence, bearing the stones on his frail body, worn with fasting [until] the Church had been repaired.

JAN. 17

Bonaventure, *The Life of St. Francis*, 2, 7

REFLECTION. The lives of the Saints are full of stories of personal humiliation.

Even after leaving all of his earthly goods, Francis endured the most difficult renunciation of all—giving up his pride.

PRAYER. *We are fools for the sake of Christ.*

(1 Cor 4:10)

 RANCIS, hearing wherein Christ gave His disciples the pattern for their life, that they should possess neither gold, nor silver, nor money for their journey, was filled with joy and said, "This is what I long for with my whole heart."

JAN. 18

Bonaventure, *The Life of St. Francis*, 3, 1

REFLECTION. Many a Saint has been given direction from the reading of Scripture—St. Anthony of the Desert, St. Augustine, St. Francis, St. Clare among others.

Truly listening and receiving the Word of God can be a life-changing experience.

PRAYER. *Indeed, the word of God is living and active.*

(Heb 4:12)

FROM this time forward, his words were **JAN.** not empty, nor for laughter, but full of **19** the might of the Holy Spirit, penetrating the heart's core, and smiting all that heard them with amazement.

Bonaventure, *The Life of St. Francis*, 3, 2

REFLECTION. As soon as Francis took that last step to final renunciation, he moved into a different place in the world that few have gone to. Mother Teresa comes to mind.

With this level of abandonment to God, the judgment ceases, and people begin to listen.

PRAYER. *Life and death are in the power of the tongue.* (Prov 18:21)

IN ALL his preaching, he would begin by **JAN.** saying: "The Lord give you peace," and he **20** preached salvation, and brought many to the true peace who were at enmity with Christ, far from salvation.

Bonaventure, *The Life of St. Francis*, 3, 2

REFLECTION. The image of the angry preacher spouting hellfire and damnation does not come out of the Catholic tradition.

Evangelism in the Catholic tradition is not rooted in strong words, but in charity and peace.

PRAYER. *How beautiful on the mountain are the feet of those who bring good news of peace and salvation.* (Isa 52:7)

S MANY recounted the truth of his simple teaching and of his life, certain of them began to turn their thoughts to penance, and, renouncing all, to join him in his habit and life.

JAN. 21

Bonaventure, *The Life of St. Francis*, 3, 3

REFLECTION. Whether you're starting a softball team, a band, or a business, getting people to join, bond, and remain can be a challenge.

True holiness and personal witness always cause people to notice and to follow.

PRAYER. *Immediately, they left their boat and their father and followed him.*

(Mt 4:22)

PRIEST of Assisi received of the Lord a vision. In a dream he beheld the whole city of Assisi beset by a great dragon. Then he saw a Cross of gold proceeding out of the mouth of Francis and the dragon was utterly put to flight.

JAN. 22

Bonaventure, *The Life of St. Francis*, 3, 5

REFLECTION. Who knows all the ways in which God communicates His plans to the world?

But it does seem that when God is moving in the world, He uses various means to communicate it to His people.

PRAYER. *In a vision the Lord said to him, "Ananias, get up and go the house of Judas and ask for Saul of Tarsus."*

(Acts 9:11)

S HE was bitterly mourning his past, the horizons of Francis' mind were enlarged, and he beheld the future of his order. Returning to the Brethren he said, "Be consoled, for God will enlarge us with the grace of His blessing."

JAN. 23

Bonaventure, *The Life of St. Francis*, 3, 6

REFLECTION. Many people have a hard time accepting that God is planning good things for their future—as if God wouldn't trust them with success.

God's plan for our future can always be trusted.

PRAYER. *For I know well the plans I have in mind for you, says the Lord. Plans for good, not evil.* (Jer 29:11)

 HEN Francis called his sons and told them many things concerning the Kingdom of God, the contempt of the world, the sacrifice of their own wills and the chastisement of the body, and his intent of sending them forth.

JAN. 24

Bonaventure, *The Life of St. Francis*, 3, 7

REFLECTION. The success of a group depends upon the willingness of the members to embrace any challenges that might face them.

With God's strength, a team so inspired can achieve anything.

PRAYER. *With God I can break through any barrier and scale any wall.* (Ps 18:30)

"G O" SAYS the sweet Father to his sons, "bring tidings of peace, and preach repentance for sins. Be patient in tribulation, watchful in prayer, zealous in toil, humble in speech, sober, and thankful."

Bonaventure, *The Life of St. Francis*, 3, 7

REFLECTION. Imagine our own lives if we could actually live out these words.

A patient, prayerful, hardworking, humble, and thankful Christian will surely make an impact on the world.

PRAYER. *Admonish the idle, support the weak, be patient, . . . pray continually, constantly give thanks.* (1 Thes 5:14-18)

 F RANCIS said unto each one singly: "Cast thy burden upon the Lord, and He shall sustain thee." He used to say these words whenever he was guiding any Brother unto obedience.

Bonaventure, *The Life of St. Francis*, 3, 7

REFLECTION. Maybe that's the secret of living this extraordinary life of sanctity—entrust it all to God.

For all the hard work the Saints do, there is a part of their lives that involves simply giving up and letting God take over.

PRAYER. *Entrust your cares to the Lord, and he will uphold you.* (Ps 55:23)

THEN knowing that he was set as an example unto the rest, he himself set forth with one companion toward one quarter of the world, the remaining six, after the fashion of a Cross, unto the other three parts.

JAN. 27

Bonaventure, *The Life of St. Francis*, 3, 7

REFLECTION. Aristotle, and Aquinas after him, spoke of the importance of finding someone to imitate in learning to live the life of the virtues.

Like being on the expressway, we're always following someone, and we're always leading someone.

PRAYER. *Do the things that you have learned, received, and heard from me and that you saw me doing.*

(Phil 4:9)

LONGING for the presence of his beloved family, with no mortal summoning, and unexpectedly, all came together as he had desired, by the working of divine goodness.

JAN. 28

Bonaventure, *The Life of St. Francis*, 3, 7

REFLECTION. When Christian friends are united in godly love through the Holy Spirit, they are led by more than mere human communication.

The one Spirit, at work in each of them, becomes their guide.

PRAYER. *And your ears shall hear a word behind you, saying, "This is the way, walk in it."*

(Isa 30:21)

N OW when the number of the Brethren was increasing, he wrote for himself and for them a Rule for their life, in simple words. Herein the observance of the Holy Gospel was set as the foundation.

JAN. 29

Bonaventure, *The Life of St. Francis*, 3, 8

REFLECTION. There is no question that humans need rules—whether on the road, in the office, or even in sports. Rules are essential.

Being intentional and structured in our prayer life, daily routine, and in forming good habits are also essential to the Christian life.

PRAYER. *Live in a manner worthy of the Lord and become fully pleasing to him.* (Col 1:10)

B UT he desired that what he had written should be approved by the Supreme Pontiff, and the Vicar of Christ, the lord Innocent the Third was disposed to give to the suppliant his fatherly sanction.

JAN. 30

Bonaventure, *The Life of St. Francis*, 3, 9

REFLECTION. To be Catholic means to be part of something larger than yourself.

Membership has its challenges and some may experience the structure as unfair, but God has ordained the Church to be His voice on earth.

PRAYER. *God has so designed the body . . . that there may be no dissension. This is the first commandment.* (1 Cor 12:24-25)

H E [Pope Innocent] delayed to perform that which the little poor one of Christ asked, by reason that to some of the Cardinals this seemed a thing untried, and too hard for human strength.

JAN.
31

Bonaventure, *The Life of St. Francis*, 3, 9

REFLECTION. We remember that God had shown Francis the vision of his Order flourishing, and now the Pope was hesitating to sanction it.

While God has only good plans for our life, He often works them out slowly, painfully slowly, in His own way.

PRAYER. *Consider it cause for great joy when you encounter various trials.* (Jas 1:2)

HE Bishop of Sabina said "If we refuse the request of this poor man as a thing too hard and untried, when his petition is the pattern of Gospel life, let us beware lest we stumble at the Gospel of Christ."

FEB.
1

Bonaventure, *The Life of St. Francis*, 3, 9

REFLECTION. It has been said that Francis' life is the fullest anyone has ever lived the Gospel. If the Bishops recognized this, they were questioning if anyone could fully live the Gospel.

Perhaps Francis is God's way of proving that living the Gospel is not impossible.

PRAYER. *Strive to be perfect, just as your heavenly Father is perfect.* (Mt 5:48)

THE successor of Peter, turning to the poor man said: "Pray my son, that He may show us His will through thee, and when we know it more surely, we will assent to thy holy desires."

FEB. 2

Bonaventure, *The Life of St. Francis*, 3, 9

REFLECTION. The patience required to submit to someone else's timetable is one of the challenges of obedience.

But if God is Lord of all, we are ultimately submitting to His perfect will working through another.

PRAYER. *Humble yourself under God's mighty hand and in due time he will raise you up.*

(1 Pet 5:6)

THE Vicar of Christ had a vision at that time. In a dream he saw the Lateran Basilica about to fall, when a little poor man, of mean stature and humble aspect, propped it with his own back.

FEB. 3

Bonaventure, *The Life of St. Francis*, 3, 10

REFLECTION. The Pope's vision echoed the words spoken to Francis from the crucifix of San Damiano—that he would rebuild the Church which was falling into ruins.

When God lays out His plan for our life, it is wonderfully confirmed in various ways.

PRAYER. *Joseph said to them, "Do not interpretations belong to God? Tell me your dreams."*

(Gen 40:8)

FRANCIS, relying on the favor of heaven and on the Papal authority, took his way with all confidence toward the valley of Spoleto, that he might both live and teach the Gospel of Christ.

FEB. 4

Bonaventure, *The Life of St. Francis*, 4, 1

REFLECTION. Francis was "relying on the favor of heaven and Papal authority."

For Catholics, it is a sweet and comforting thing to be blessed by God and in harmony with His Church on earth.

PRAYER. *God's household, that is, the Church of the Living God, the pillar and bulwark of the truth.* (1 Tim 3:15)

 HE WAS conversing with his companions on the road when they found themselves wearied and hungry in a deserted place. Suddenly there appeared a man carrying bread, which he gave them, then suddenly vanished.

FEB. 5

Bonaventure, *The Life of St. Francis*, 4,1

REFLECTION. This experience on the way back from Rome confirmed two things.

The Cardinals were right that this Franciscan way of poverty was humanly impossible. And secondly, that God would make it possible for the sake of living the Gospel perfectly.

PRAYER. *He took the bread and gave it to them. Then their eyes were opened . . . but he vanished from their sight.* (Lk 24:30-31)

THEY began to discuss whether to live among men or in deserted places. Francis was illumined by a divine oracle that he was sent to win souls that the devil was eager to carry off, and he chose to live for men rather than self.

FEB. 6

Bonaventure, *The Life of St. Francis*, 4, 2

REFLECTION. One can achieve holiness and fight the devil in solitude or among men.

Both the hermit and the businessman will wrestle with the devil in the flesh and in the spirit.

PRAYER. *May you be fortified with the strength that comes from his glorious power.* (Col 1:11)

THE man of God returned with his companions to a certain hut near Assisi where they lived in much toil and necessity, seeking to be refreshed rather with the bread of tears than of luxury.

FEB. 7

Bonaventure, *The Life of St. Francis*, 4, 3

REFLECTION. When love is deep and true, there is a joy in suffering for the beloved. Caring for a newborn or a sick child can be an example of this.

Perhaps the Saint is someone who loves God and all His creatures constantly with this kind of love.

PRAYER. *It is only right for me to feel this way for you, because I hold you in my heart.*

(Phil 1:7)

HEY had not yet any ecclesiastical books wherein they might chant the Canonical Hours. In place of such, they meditated day and night on the Cross of Christ, continuously looking at it.

Bonaventure, *The Life of St. Francis*, 4, 3

REFLECTION. The Catholic faith is rich with statuary, imagery, and architecture. Often called a sermon in stone, these images teach us in ways that no human words can.

A house filled with such imagery is part of handing on the Catholic faith to family and friends.

PRAYER. *Eyes to see and ears to hear, both are gifts from the Lord.* (Prov 20:12)

HE Brethren sought him to teach them to pray. He said: "When you pray, say 'We adore Thee, O Christ, in all Thy churches in the whole world, for by Thy holy Cross Thou hast redeemed the world.'"

Bonaventure, *The Life of St. Francis*, 4, 3

REFLECTION. This prayer of Francis points to three things: Christ, His presence in the Church on earth, and the sacrifice on the Cross.

All of these are most perfectly present and summed up in the Mass, for which Francis had a special devotion.

PRAYER. *Blessed are those who are invited to the wedding banquet of the Lamb.* (Rev 19:9)

OREOVER, he taught them to praise God in all things and through all His creatures.

Bonaventure, *The Life of St. Francis*, 4, 3

REFLECTION. There is a comprehensive loving embrace of absolutely everything in the Franciscan way.

While some find God in the Church and sacred things and some find God in nature, Francis saw God everywhere.

PRAYER. *Where could I go to hide from your spirit? Where can I flee from your presence?*

(Ps 139:7)

 HE holy man began to scrutinize the secret things of their consciences, to console them with that marvelous vision, and to foretell many things that should come to pass concerning the progress of the Order.

Bonaventure, *The Life of St. Francis*, 4, 4

REFLECTION. There are so many things we don't understand about life, especially about the inner workings of our own self and our future path.

But God, in His omniscience, knows all of these things. In His love, He works them all together for our good.

PRAYER. *For we know that God makes all things work together for good.* *(Rom 8:28)*

S HE revealed things surpassing mortal sense, the Brethren perceived that the Spirit of the Lord had rested upon Francis in such fullness that they would walk securely in following his teaching and life.

FEB. 12

Bonaventure, *The Life of St. Francis*, 4, 4

REFLECTION. We all have our secrets in that inner life that we feel no one knows.

But God knows even that part of us, and may reveal it to the Saints for the purpose of confirming His presence by sharing something only He could know.

PRAYER. *Come see a man who told me everything I ever did.* (Jn 4:29)

OW as time went by, and the Brethren were multiplied, their watchful shepherd began to call them into Chapters, dividing them an inheritance of poverty and to each his portion of obedience.

FEB. 13

Bonaventure, *The Life of St. Francis*, 4, 10

REFLECTION. Here is the moment when the Franciscan order shows it is truly of God, that in success it remains focused on poverty and obedience.

How many gifted celebrities, athletes, or businessmen have been crushed by the weight of success?

PRAYER. *Some people have ignored their conscience and destroyed their faith.* (1 Tim 1:19)

HEN Francis perceived that by his example many were incited to bear the Cross of Christ with fervor, he himself was inspired to reach for the palm of victory by the heights of unconquered valor. **FEB. 14**

Bonaventure, *The Life of St. Francis*, 5, 1

REFLECTION. Despite all of the focus on renunciation in the life of Francis and many of the Saints, there is, at the same time an insatiable appetite to do more.

St. Ignatius of Loyola, the founder of the Society of Jesus, and his followers embraced the practice of *magis*—doing "more" for the glory of God.

PRAYER. *So you knew that I reap where I have not sown and gather where I have not scattered!* (Mt 25:26)

 E RESTRAINED his sensual appetites with such discipline that he would barely take what was necessary to support life. **FEB. 15**

Bonaventure, *The Life of St. Francis*, 5, 1

REFLECTION. Each Christian is called to live the fullness of his faith in the state he is given.

Not all can follow Francis' example completely. Although all can benefit from periodic fasting and small daily mortifications.

PRAYER. *So we fasted and implored our God for this, and he listened to our entreaty.* (Ezr 8:23)

HE USED to say that it was difficult to satisfy the needs of the body without yielding to the inclinations of the senses.

FEB. 16

Bonaventure, *The Life of St. Francis*, 5, 1

REFLECTION. Certainly Francis was on to something in recognizing how the harmless leads to the harmful.

A glass or two of wine and soon we're eating more than we want and saying more than we should.

PRAYER. *The drunkard and the glutton will come to poverty, and slumber will clothe them with rags.* (Prov 23:21)

HE WOULD seldom allow himself cooked food, and, when he did, he... would as far as possible destroy its savor and taste.

FEB. 17

Bonaventure, *The Life of St. Francis*, 5, 1

REFLECTION. All the salt, sugar, and sauce we add to our food has the effect of covering up a more subtle, natural taste that we have lost the ability to appreciate.

Similarly, luxury and entertainment are covering up a more subtle, natural experience that we have lost the ability to perceive.

PRAYER. *I said in my heart, "Come now, I will test you with pleasure; enjoy yourself." But behold, this also was vanity.* (Eccl 2:1-2)

E WAS always discovering methods of more rigorous abstinence, and would daily make progress in their use, like a novice, ever making trial of some new method of chastising the lusts of the flesh.

FEB. 18

Bonaventure, *The Life of St. Francis*, 5, 1

REFLECTION. The amazing thing about your body is that it will get used to whatever you give it.

We can exercise and eat healthy food, or eat and drink too much and suffer the consequences. This is why it is so important to form good habits.

PRAYER. *They promise freedom, but they themselves are slaves of corruption. For people are slaves to whatever has mastered them.* (2 Pet 2:19)

 HEN he went abroad he adapted himself to them that entertained him. In this way he showed himself gracious toward his neighbor, and in all things subject to the Gospel of Christ.

FEB. 19

Bonaventure, *The Life of St. Francis*, 5, 1

REFLECTION. Living for Christ often sets us apart from the crowd, but it does not give us permission to inconvenience the crowd.

Christianity should never be an excuse to be uncharitable.

PRAYER. *Eat and drink whatever is offered to you.* (Lk 10:7)

HE bare ground served as a couch to his wearied body, and he would often sleep sitting..., clad in one poor tunic. He served the Lord in cold and nakedness.

FEB. 20

Bonaventure, *The Life of St. Francis*, 5, 1

REFLECTION. What is this connection between self-denial and holiness?

Perhaps pleasure feeds the ego, and the ego turns us in on ourselves and makes it difficult to live for God and others in true charity.

PRAYER. *For the grace of God has appeared, . . . training us to renounce worldly passions, and to live self-controlled, upright, and godly lives.*

(Tit 2:11-12)

E ABHORRED softness in clothing, and loved harshness. He had learned by sure experience that the devils fear hardness, but that by luxury and softness they are the more keenly incited to tempt men.

FEB. 21

Bonaventure, *The Life of St. Francis*, 5, 2

REFLECTION. People today are aware of the value of exercise to stay in shape.

For Francis, spiritual exercises were more important. The stakes are so much higher now.

PRAYER. *While physical training has some value, the benefits of godliness are unlimited, since it holds out promise not only for this life, but also for the life to come.* (1 Tim 4:8)

34

HE TAUGHT the Brothers zealously to shun sloth, as the repository of all evil thoughts, showing by his example that the rebellious and idle body must be subdued by unceasing discipline and profitable toil.

FEB.
22

Bonaventure, *The Life of St. Francis*, 5, 6

REFLECTION. It has often been said that "Idle hands are the devil's workshop."

From the day that God set Adam and Eve in the garden to tend it, productive work has been shown to be a good use of one's time.

PRAYER. *Then the LORD God took the man and put him into the garden of Eden to cultivate it and watch over it.* (Gen 2:15)

HE OFTEN said: "Would that my Brethren should labor and employ themselves, lest, being given up to sloth, they should stray into sins of heart or tongue."

FEB.
23

Bonaventure, *The Life of St. Francis*, 5, 6

REFLECTION. We live in an age of such affluence that our work is often seen as a burden or an interruption.

Jesus' life on earth was spent constantly working and praying. Even now He continues His work in the Church, along with His Father and the Holy Spirit.

PRAYER. *My father is always working, and so am I.* (Jn 5:17)

35

FRANCIS taught that a Gospel silence should be observed by the Brethren, that they should at all times diligently refrain from every idle word, as those that shall give account on the Day of Judgment. **FEB. 24**

Bonaventure, *The Life of St. Francis*, 5, 6

REFLECTION. God has given us a tremendous power in the use of speech and language. It is easy to take it for granted, but notice that we are the only creatures who can talk.

Being mindful of our words and maintaining silence require constant vigilance.

PRAYER. *On the day of judgment people will have to account for every careless word they utter.* *(Mt 12:36)*

ALTHOUGH he sought with all his might to lead the Brethren to the austere life, yet severity without discretion pleased him not. He taught them to follow prudence as the charioteer of the virtues. **FEB. 25**

Admonitions, 18

REFLECTION. When Francis sensed that a brother's fasting was a danger to his health, he would sit down and share some bread with him.

His example showed that loving concern is the greatest of all sacrifices.

PRAYER. *Stop drinking only water. Take a little wine for your stomach and your frequent ailments.* *(1 Tim 5:23)*

UMILITY, the guardian and glory of all virtues, abounded in rich fullness in the man of God. In his own estimation, he was naught but a sinner, whereas in truth he was the mirror of all saintliness.

Bonaventure, *The Life of St. Francis*, 6, 1

REFLECTION. Why would a Saint claim to be a sinner?

It might be that he is not comparing himself to us, but to a much higher standard, by which we may not even chart!

PRAYER. *But they will give account to him who is ready to judge the living and the dead.* (1 Pet 4:5)

 FTEN when folk exalted the merits of his saintliness, he would bid one of the Brethren to pour contemptuous words into his ears. When that Brother whispered "Lazy beggar," he would rejoice in spirit.

Bonaventure, *The Life of St. Francis*, 6, 1

REFLECTION. One might call Francis' efforts to remain holy "strategic." He did not plod along seeing what would come next. He foresaw dangers to his spirit and he made plans to fight it.

Each Christian should live with that forethought to avoid sin and practice virtue.

PRAYER. *Which one of you, intending to build a tower, would not first sit down and estimate the cost?* (Lk 14:28)

HEN he was glorified by many, he would say: "Praise me not as one that is safe. No man should be praised before his end be known."

FEB.
28

Bonaventure, *The Life of St. Francis*, 6, 3

REFLECTION. As long as we live in this mortal body on earth, we can change. Nothing is certain. The cement is still wet.

Francis was keenly aware of the importance of taking nothing for granted.

PRAYER. *It is not that I have already attained the goal or reached perfection, but I press on. . . . I do not claim to have taken hold of it yet.*

(Phil 3:12-13)

 OW this Gospel merchant,—that he might in many ways make a profit—preferred not so much to be set in authority as to be set under authority, not so much to command as to obey.

FEB.
29

Bonaventure, *The Life of St. Francis*, 6, 4

REFLECTION. It is curious that St. Bonaventure described Francis in business terms.

Francis saw more value to our spirit in obedience than in giving orders. Surely that was because obedience requires more humility.

PRAYER. *For everyone who exalts himself will be humbled, and he who humbles himself will be exalted.*

(Lk 14:11)

WHEN asked what kind of man **MAR.** should be esteemed truly obedient, he said, "A dead body. Lift up **1** a dead body, and place it where thou will. Thou shall see it will not complain of where it is set."

Bonaventure, *The Life of St. Francis*, 6, 4

REFLECTION. This striking example of obedience underscores the need to die to self.

Our ego wants to possess, consume, and control. Only by letting our ego "die" can we be brought back to life.

PRAYER. *Brothers, I proclaim by my pride in you, which I have in Christ Jesus our Lord, I die every day!* (1 Cor 15:31)

 HE SAID once to his companion: "In ex- **MAR.** alted places there is the danger of falling, in the humility of a submissive **2** spirit there is profit. Why then do we look for perils rather than profits?"

Bonaventure, *The Life of St. Francis*, 6, 5

REFLECTION. The old saying goes, "Uneasy lies the head that wears the crown." The king was always in fear of his life.

The saying is true of temporal power, and it is equally true of the spirit. The more we are praised, the more danger we bring to our souls.

PRAYER. *Pride goes before destruction, and an arrogant spirit before a fall.* (Prov 16:18)

ROM this same reason of humility, Francis was minded that his Brethren should be called by the name of Minors, that his followers might know from their very name that they had come to learn humility.

Bonaventure, *The Life of St. Francis*, 6, 5

REFLECTION. We've often seen the letters O.F.M. after a Franciscan's name. It stands for "Order of Friars Minor."

Francis' only desire was to be small. This "downward mobility" is a trademark of all the Saints.

PRAYER. *The greatest among you must be your servant.* (Mt 23:11)

 HEN the Bishop inquired if his Brethren should be promoted to high places, Francis said: "Lord, If you desire that they should bear fruit, keep them in the state of their calling, and let them not rise to leadership."

Bonaventure, *The Life of St. Francis*, 6, 5

REFLECTION. Only four Franciscan friars have risen to the rank of Pope, and most of them against their own wishes.

For the Franciscans, their leadership will always be by example, rather than by title or rank.

PRAYER. *Each person should remain in the state wherein he was called.* (1 Cor 7:20)

NOW since he set humility before all honors, in himself and in his followers, God, Who loves the humble, deemed him worthy of loftier heights.

MAR. 5

Bonaventure, *The Life of St. Francis*, 6, 6

REFLECTION. A key life lesson we all learn eventually: the more self-sufficient you try to be, the more people want to help you.

As Mother Teresa has shown us, true humility somehow leads to exaltation.

PRAYER. *My friend, move up to a higher place.*

(Lk 14:10)

 A BROTHER, falling into an ecstasy, beheld among many seats in heaven one that was more honorable than the rest. As he considered, he heard a voice saying: "This seat is kept for the humble Francis."

MAR. 6

Bonaventure, *The Life of St. Francis*, 6, 6

REFLECTION. Francis avoided being singled out or given any special treatment during his lifetime, but in heaven Francis would be honored for a lifetime of giving glory to God.

Scenes of heaven in the Book of Revelation show the Saints exhibiting humility even there.

PRAYER. *They cast down their crowns before the throne and cry out, "Worthy are you, O Lord our God."*

(Rev 4:10-11)

HEN the Brother inquired what he thought of himself, Francis said, "If any man had received such mercy from Christ as I, I think he would have been far more acceptable to God than I."

Bonaventure, *The Life of St. Francis*, 6, 6

MAR. 7

REFLECTION. Even when we deem someone to be great or holy, we cannot know the whole story.

Jesus does make it clear that judgment will be graded upon what He has given us by nature and grace.

PRAYER. *Even more will be asked of a person to whom more has been entrusted.* (Lk 12:48)

 E ALSO said, "He that would attain this height must in all ways renounce the wisdom of the world and even knowledge of letters, so that he may go in the strength of the Lord."

Bonaventure, *The Life of St. Francis*, 7, 2

MAR. 8

REFLECTION. To give up learning as a form of self-denial is truly a radical sense of poverty.

Yet, Francis knew that for monks learning was all they had, and often became a source of pride. Not only material possessions get in the way of holiness.

PRAYER. *And those who make use of the world as though they had no dealings with the world.*
(1 Cor 7:31)

ET all anxious thoughts be removed from the poor ones of Christ. Nothing in creation will refuse its service to those who have left all for the Creator of all.

MAR. 9

Bonaventure, *The Life of St. Francis*, 7, 2

REFLECTION. As hard as Francis tried to not be fed or clothed or housed, he always had more than he wanted.

The ongoing success of his order is further proof that completely trusting God will somehow be rewarded.

PRAYER. *Consider the generations long past and see: has anyone trusted in the Lord and been disappointed? Has anyone persevered in his fear and been forsaken?* *(Sir 2:10)*

 CCORDINGLY, he would say that that preacher should be deplored who in his preaching did not seek the salvation of souls, but his own glory.

MAR. 10

Bonaventure, *The Life of St. Francis*, 7, 2

REFLECTION. Whereas ministry work should be done for God's glory and our own salvation, it often seems to get switched around.

It is easy to be "holy" in order to "help God" while making ourselves look good.

PRAYER. *Do not act out of selfish ambition or vanity.* *(Phil 2:3)*

43

ITH heartfelt piety and glowing zeal he sought the salvation of souls. He was filled with the sweetest fragrance whenever he heard of many being led to the truth by the repute of the holy Brethren.

MAR. 11

Bonaventure, *The Life of St. Francis*, 7, 3

REFLECTION. For Francis, all this radical holiness was directed toward one thing only, the salvation of souls.

In this "live and let live" culture, it is hard to fulfill the great commission to lead others to salvation.

PRAYER. *Go, therefore, and make disciples of all nations.* (Mt 28:19)

 EARING such reports, he would rejoice in spirit, heaping with blessings most worthy of all acceptance those Brethren who, by word or deed, were bringing sinners to the love of Christ.

MAR. 12

Bonaventure, *The Life of St. Francis*, 7, 3

REFLECTION. Note that sinners were brought to Christ by word and deed—that is, by example.

It is sometimes hard to appreciate that what we do actually influences others more than what we say.

PRAYER. *The Son can do nothing by himself. He can do only what he sees the Father doing.* (Jn 5:19)

IKEWISE, those who were transgressing **MAR.** against holy Religion by their evil works, fell under the heaviest sentence of his curse. "Be they accursed who by their evil example destroy that which Thou has built up."

MAR. 13

Bonaventure, *The Life of St. Francis*, 7, 3

REFLECTION. Whether or not human beings are related to monkeys, we cannot deny that human beings are imitators. We imitate the good; we imitate the bad.

This is why Jesus was especially harsh to those who gave bad example.

PRAYER. *Woe to the world because of scandals. . . . woe to the one through whom they come.*

(Mt 18:7)

FTEN he was affected by such sadness, by reason of the stumbling-block to the weak Brethren, that his strength would have failed him, had he not been sustained by the comfort of the Divine mercy.

MAR. 14

Bonaventure, *The Life of St. Francis*, 6, 4

REFLECTION. That someone should hinder the spiritual progress of another is truly sad to those who love holiness.

This is ironic, because such sin is usually undertaken in pursuit of happiness. But what seems a joy is really a sorrow.

PRAYER. *Woe to you who laugh now, for you will mourn and weep.*

(Lk 6:25)

NCE when he was disquieted because of evil examples, he heard from the Lord: "Why fret, poor little mortal? Have I set thee as shepherd over My Religion that thou should forget I am its chief Protector? I will keep it and feed it. It shall always abide under My guard."

Bonaventure, *The Life of St. Francis*, 8, 3

REFLECTION. Even Francis needed to be reminded that, in the end, it all belongs to God; it is His world, and His responsibility.

PRAYER. *I, myself, will be the shepherd of my sheep ... says the Lord.* (Ezek 34:15)

HE vice of slander Francis would shrink from as a serpent's tooth declaring it to be a hateful plague, as the slanderer feeds on the blood of those souls that he has slain by his tongue.

Bonaventure, *The Life of St. Francis*, 8, 4

REFLECTION. We use words so often and for so many purposes that it is easy to underestimate their power.

Francis saw the harmful effect of slander and reacted forcefully against it.

PRAYER. *Whoever goes about slandering reveals secrets, but he who is trustworthy in spirit keeps a confidence.* (Prov 11:13)

"THE sin of slanderers," he would say, **MAR.** "is more heinous than that of robbers, inasmuch as the law of Christ binds us to desire more the salvation of the soul than of the body." **17**

Bonaventure, *The Life of St. Francis*, 8, 4

REFLECTION. We hear children say that "sticks and stones may break my bones but names will never hurt me."

Perhaps we should teach them that there is more danger to the soul of the bully and name-caller than there is to the victim.

PRAYER. *Speak evil of no one, avoid quarreling, be gentle, and show perfect courtesy toward all people.*

(Tit 3:2)

HE CAME on a great flock of sheep in **MAR.** the pastures. And when he had given them gracious greeting they left their **18** feeding, and all ran toward him, raising their heads, and gazing fixedly on him with their eyes.

Bonaventure, *The Life of St. Francis*, 6, 4

REFLECTION. Somehow, by giving up everything he owned, Francis came into deeper contact with everything that existed.

This must be what the Bible means that one has to give up everything to gain everything.

PRAYER. *When he discovered a pearl of great value, he sold everything he owned and bought it!*

(Mt 13:46)

47

LAMB was brought to the man of **MAR. 19**
God. The holy man exhorted the
lamb to be diligent in the divine
praises; the lamb would enter the
church and bend the knee, bleating
before the altar of the Virgin
Mother.

Bonaventure, *The Life of St. Francis*, 8, 7

REFLECTION. Animals, like humans, are imitators and they learn by observing.

Francis' witness was so authentic, and his influence so powerful, that it even held sway over animals.

PRAYER. *All your works shall praise you, O LORD.* *(Ps 145:10)*

 URTHERMORE, at the consecration of the **MAR. 20**
most holy Body of Christ in the Mass, it
would bend its knees and bow, as though
this sheep would reprove human irreverence, and inspire Christ's devout to revere the Sacrament.

Bonaventure, *The Life of St. Francis*, 8, 7

REFLECTION. As human beings learn from watching, so nature has a lot to teach us.

But when nature teaches us something that should belong uniquely to us as humans, it is a humiliating rebuke.

PRAYER. *But Balaam was stopped from his madness when his donkey—a dumb creature—rebuked him with a human voice.* *(2 Pet 2:16)*

WHEN he had come to the solitude of Alverna, birds of diverse sort... seemed by their tuneful chorus and joyous movements to rejoice at his coming and to invite the holy Father to tarry there.

MAR. 21

Bonaventure, *The Life of St. Francis*, 8, 10

REFLECTION. Human beings have always been fascinated with the flight of birds. The ancients studied birds' movements for signs and omens.

Perhaps, like Francis, we are mystified by their angelic qualities, borne on the wind, with wings, and always singing.

PRAYER. *The heavens were opened and the Spirit of God was seen descending in the form of a dove and coming to rest on him.* (Mt 3:16)

OF THE ardent love that glowed in Francis, who can tell? He seemed utterly consumed, like a coal that is set on fire, by the flame of the love divine.

MAR. 22

Bonaventure, *The Life of St. Francis*, 9, 1

REFLECTION. The Holy Spirit comes down "like tongues of flame" upon the disciples, and their hearts are "burning within them" as they speak with Jesus on the road to Emmaus.

The heat and energy of a fire is a fitting image for God being present to us.

PRAYER. *His message becomes like a fire locked up inside of me, burning in my heart and soul.*

(Jer 20:9)

FOR, at the mere mention of the love of the Lord, he was aroused, moved, and enkindled, as though the inner chords of his heart vibrated under the bow of the voice from without.

MAR. 23

Bonaventure, *The Life of St. Francis*, 9, 1

REFLECTION. Music, like the sea and the sky, has something of eternity about it.

Who would be surprised to learn that in heaven, the Angels don't merely speak in monotones, but they sing their sentences to each other with beautiful melodies?

PRAYER. *Addressing one another in psalms and hymns and spiritual songs, singing and making melody to the Lord with your heart.* (Eph 5:19)

THAT he might by all things be stirred up unto the divine love, he rejoiced in all the works of the Lord's hands, and through the sight of their joy was up-lifted unto their life-giving cause and origin.

MAR. 24

Bonaventure, *The Life of St. Francis*, 9, 1

REFLECTION. One can usually find something to be sad about, and one can usually find something to be happy about. It often depends upon your mood and how you react.

Choosing to be hopeful at a difficult time takes courage.

PRAYER. *I perceived that there is nothing better for man than to be joyful and to do good as long as he lives.* (Eccl 3:12)

FRANCIS beheld in fair things Him Who is the most fair, and, through traces of God imprinted on His creatures, he followed on to reach the Beloved, making of all things a ladder whereby he might ascend to Him. **MAR. 25**

Bonaventure, *The Life of St. Francis*, 6, 4

REFLECTION. So much that is beautiful in this world becomes an anchor to us, creating short term desire and lust for material things.

Francis took the opposite path, using the goods of God's creation as a ladder to climb to higher things.

PRAYER. *Set your minds on things that are above, not on things that are on earth.* (Col 3:2)

WITH such glowing love he was moved toward Christ that it seemed to the servant of God that he felt his Savior almost continually present before his eyes, as he once revealed to his companions. **MAR. 26**

Bonaventure, *The Life of St. Francis*, 9, 2

REFLECTION. Saints seem to experience the benefits of heaven already on earth.

The companionship of Christ is something that we can all know through faith, for Christ is always with us.

PRAYER. *Fear thou not, for I am with you; be not dismayed, for I am your God; I will strengthen you and I will help you.* (Isa 41:10)

TOWARD the Sacrament of the Lord's Body he felt a glowing devotion that consumed the very marrow of his bones, marvelling with utmost amazement at that most loving condescension.

MAR. 27

Bonaventure, *The Life of St. Francis*, 6, 4

REFLECTION. Vatican II declares the Eucharist the source and summit of our faith. As a devout Christian, Francis knew this.

Just as Francis always saw Christ before his eyes, so he often received Christ in his physical body.

PRAYER. *Jesus said to them, "Amen, amen, I say to you, unless you eat the flesh of the Son of Man and drink his blood, you do not have life within you."* (Jn 6:53)

HE LOVED with an unspeakable affection the Mother of the Lord Jesus Christ. In her, after Christ, he put his chief trust, making her his own patron and that of his Brethren.

MAR. 28

Bonaventure, *The Life of St. Francis*, 9, 3

REFLECTION. In a binary movement, devotion to Mary brings us closer to Jesus, and devotion to Jesus leads us closer to Mary.

As our true mother, Mary's ability to intercede for us is powerful indeed.

PRAYER. *When the wine ran out, the mother of Jesus said to him, "They have no wine."* (Jn 2:3)

E WAS bound by ties of inseparable affection to the Angelic spirits that do glow with wondrous fire to approach God, and out of devotion to them he would fast for forty days.

MAR. 29

Bonaventure, *The Life of St. Francis*, 9, 3

REFLECTION. The ministry of the Angels is one of the mysteries of life. In the interplay between the spirit and the material world, Angels are the conduit.

They watch over us with special devotion and care.

PRAYER. *The angel of the Lord encamps around those who fear him, to deliver them from harm.* (Ps 34:7)

 S HE called to remembrance all the Saints, he was kindled afresh with the flame of heavenly love; he regarded with the utmost devotion all the Apostles, and especially Peter and Paul.

MAR. 30

Bonaventure, *The Life of St. Francis*, 9, 3

REFLECTION. The Church's constant remembrance of the Saints, study of their lives, and beseeching their intercession gives us a powerful example for holiness.

Such is the purpose of this book!

PRAYER. *Here is a call for the endurance of the saints, those who keep the commandments of God and remain faithful to Jesus.* (Rev. 14:12)

OW this exceeding devotion of love uplifted him into the divine in such a way as that his loving goodwill extended to those that had received with him a like nature and grace.

MAR. 31

Bonaventure, *The Life of St. Francis*, 9, 4

REFLECTION. Bonaventure relates, in order of importance, Francis' devotion to Christ, the Eucharist, the Virgin Mary, Angels, and the Saints (reflections March 26-30).

As Catholics, these are the treasured means by which we enter into the divine life.

PRAYER. *Stand firm, brethern, and hold fast to the traditions that you have been taught.* (2 Thes 2:15)

 E WOULD say that nothing was to be preferred before the salvation of souls, proving this chiefly by the fact that the Only-Begotten Son of God deigned to hang on the Cross for the sake of men's souls.

APR. 1

Bonaventure, *The Life of St. Francis*, 9, 4

REFLECTION. In this world, there are so many things we could do with our time. And though we must work, most of us have plenty of spare time. It's all about priorities.

For St. Francis, his priority was saving souls.

PRAYER. *The aim of this instruction is love that derives from a pure heart, a good conscience, and a sincere faith.* (1 Tim 1:5)

54

E EMULATED, with an ardent flame of love, the glorious victory of the holy Martyrs. Kindled by that perfect love that casts out fear, he yearned to offer himself up to the Lord in martyrdom.

Bonaventure, *The Life of St. Francis 9, 6*

REFLECTION. When we think about how completely St. Francis was sold on God, it is no surprise that he wanted the ultimate sacrifice of martyrdom.

Though not all the Saints are martyrs, all the Saints longed to give the ultimate sacrifice for God.

PRAYER. *My desire is to depart and to be with Christ.*

(Phil 1:23)

HEN the man of God,—perceiving that his life in the body was still needed for the family that he had begotten—returned to feed the sheep that had been committed to his care.

Bonaventure, *The Life of St. Francis, 9, 6*

REFLECTION. The desire for martyrdom in many Saints was never fulfilled.

And thus, the fact that they are not allowed to die for love of God becomes one of the greatest sacrifices they can make for Him.

PRAYER. *For me to live is Christ and to die is gain.*

(Phil 1:21)

RANCIS, feeling himself in the body to be absent from the Lord, and that he might not be without his Beloved, prayed without ceasing to be present with God in Spirit.

APR. 4

Bonaventure, *The Life of St. Francis*, 10, 1

REFLECTION. So if the Saint is denied the grace of martyrdom, and the perfect union in heaven to which it leads, their love drives them to find another way to be united to God.

St. Francis used prayer as a means to be constantly in the divine presence.

PRAYER. *In all of your prayers and entreaties, pray always in the Spirit.* (Eph 6:18)

 RAYER was a consolation to him, being already made a fellow-citizen with the Angels in the heavenly mansions. With ardent yearning he sought his Beloved, separated only by the wall of the flesh.

APR. 5

Bonaventure, *The Life of St. Francis*, 10, 1

REFLECTION. Like anything else, prayer is something that we can get better at and improve upon.

The Saints prayed constantly, until they prayed so perfectly that they were present with God as much as is possible while still on earth.

PRAYER. *Then Jesus told them a parable about the need for them to pray always and never to lose heart.* (Lk 18:1)

56

FTEN he was rapt in such ecstasies of contemplation as that he was carried out of himself, and, while perceiving things beyond mortal sense, knew nothing of what was happening in the world around him.

**APR.
6**

Bonaventure, *The Life of St. Francis*, 10, 2

REFLECTION. Francis' spiritual union with God was so complete that the flesh would become as if dead while he was out of the body, communing with his Beloved.

St. Paul also wrote about this experience.

PRAYER. *I know a man in Christ who . . . was caught up into the third heaven . . . whether in the body or out of the body, I cannot say.*

(2 Cor 12:2)

IN ALL that he did, distrusting his own working, and relying on the heavenly goodness, he cast all his care upon the Lord in earnest prayer.

**APR.
7**

Bonaventure, *The Life of St. Francis*, 10, 1

REFLECTION. For all the willpower and self-denial that Francis showed, he never forgot that it was God at work in him through the Holy Spirit that made his holiness possible.

And since it was God's action and Francis' co-operation with His grace that caused such holiness, then each of us has a shot at sainthood too.

PRAYER. *Passing into holy souls from age to age [the Spirit of Wisdom] produces friends of God and prophets.*

(Wis 7:27)

NE Lent, he had made a little vase, that he might fill up his spare moments, and they not be utterly wasted.

APR. 8

Bonaventure, *The Life of St. Francis*, 10, 6

REFLECTION. The Saints all had this in common—they made the most of every moment they were given. They never wasted time.

Ironically, it seems the more firmly one believes in the next world, the more passionately one fights to make the most of every moment in this present world.

PRAYER. *Take care to live as intelligent people. . . . Make the most of the present time.* (Eph 5:15)

HREE years before his death he was inspired to celebrate the memory of the Birth of the Child Jesus, for the kindling of devotion. He made ready a manger, and brought hay, together with an ox and an ass.

APR. 9

Bonaventure, *The Life of St. Francis*, 10, 7

REFLECTION. Francis is credited with initiating the custom of setting up a manger scene that we have all come to associate with Christmas.

This is just one way that Catholics are urged to enter into the life of Christ, which we do in a supreme way when we enter into His death at Mass.

PRAYER. *Do you not know that all of us who have been baptized in Christ Jesus were baptized into his death?* (Rom 6:3)

NTO such a tranquillity of mind had his
zeal for prayer and practice of virtue
brought the man of God that he searched
the deep things of the Scriptures with
marvelous intellectual discernment.

Bonaventure, *The Life of St. Francis*, 11, 1

REFLECTION. Francis' life was an amazing reflection of the Gospel, but he could never attain
that unless he had actually read—and meditated—upon the Gospel.

We also benefit from spending time reading
the Bible on our own.

PRAYER. *Man does not live by bread alone, but
by every word that comes forth from the
mouth of God.*

(Mt 4:4)

 E WOULD read the sacred books,
and whatever had once been presented to his mind became indelibly
imprinted on his memory, for he
comprehended by hearing and by an
attentive mind.

Bonaventure, *The Life of St. Francis*, 11, 1

REFLECTION. God has given us many tools and
gifts to know him better. Among these are in-
tellect, memory, and concentration.

Those who strive for holiness use these gifts
to draw closer to God.

PRAYER. *This Book of the Law shall not depart
from your mouth, but you shall meditate on it
day and night, so that you may be careful to do
all that is written in it.*

(Jos 1:8)

OR was it unfitting that he should **APR.** receive from God an understanding of the Scriptures, for by the imita- **12** tion of Christ he set forth and ful- filled in his deeds their perfect truth.

Bonaventure, *The Life of St. Francis*, 11, 2

REFLECTION. Francis understood Scriptures not only because he read them, but mostly because he lived them.

We do not think ourselves into right action as much as we act ourselves into right thinking.

PRAYER. *Be doers of the Word and not just hearers who only deceive themselves.* (Jas 1:22)

 O MIGHTILY did the spirit of prophecy **APR.** shine forth in him that he both knew **13** what was to come, and beheld the se- crets of men's hearts, and perceived ab- sent things as though they were present.

Bonaventure, *The Life of St. Francis*, 11, 3

REFLECTION. Like many of the Saints, Francis had deep wisdom and knowledge of things beyond what is natural to most.

Perhaps it is only when one's entire life becomes oriented to serve others, to forget self, and to imitate God that this kind of knowledge can be attained.

PRAYER. *And who could ever have known your will, had you not given Wisdom and sent your holy Spirit from above?* (Wis 9:17)

E SEEMED to have approached the mirror of eternal light to gaze therein, and by its wondrous radiance the sight of his mind perceived things that were absent in bodily form as though they were present.

Bonaventure, *The Life of St. Francis*, 11, 10

REFLECTION. The ability to read the hearts of others and to predict the future is common to some of the Saints.

Certain Saints demonstrate powers bestowed on them by God for His greater glory. Such gifts are open to some through a total sacrifice of self to God.

PRAYER. *Do nothing out of selfish ambition or vanity, but humbly regard others as better than yourselves.* (Phil 2:3)

 HE most exalted Teacher wants to reveal His mysteries to the babes and the simple, such as a shepherd, a fisherman, and lastly a merchant when he had sold and disposed of all things for the sake of Christ.

Bonaventure, *The Life of St. Francis*, 11, 14

REFLECTION. We are used to the idea that God chooses fishermen to do His will, but it is interesting to note that Francis was a businessman.

When God looks for one who is simple and humble, that description applies to their spirit more than their state in life, as the many kings and queens who have become Saints attests.

PRAYER. *God resists the proud, but he gives grace to the humble.* (Jas 4:6)

H E WAS in the habit of inquiring after what way and manner of life he might most perfectly serve God according to His will. This was his highest philosophy, this his highest desire, so long as he lived.

APR. **16**

Bonaventure, *The Life of St. Francis*, 12, 2

REFLECTION. It is common to daydream about winning the lottery, or taking a dream vacation, or living in the perfect house.

For St. Francis, his daydreams were about perfectly knowing and doing the will of God.

PRAYER. *Try to learn what pleases God.*

(Eph 5:10)

H E WAS about to preach in the presence of the Pope and found that he had forgotten all he had prepared. He invoked the Holy Spirit and began to pour forth words of such power that it was clearly not him that spoke, but the Spirit of the Lord.

APR. **17**

Bonaventure, *The Life of St. Francis*, 12, 7

REFLECTION. This episode in the life of Francis was further proof that a man on his own can do nothing. Francis had prepared ahead of time, but he was beset by an attack of nerves.

Only when he invoked the Holy Spirit was he able to speak as a true Saint.

PRAYER. *I will give you words and wisdom that none will be able to contradict.*

(Lk 21:15)

I T WAS not his way to smooth over the faults of any, but to smite them, nor to flatter the life of sinners, but rather to aim at it with stern reproofs. Unto great and small alike he spoke with the same firm spirit.

Bonaventure, *The Life of St. Francis*, 12, 8

REFLECTION. Modern psychology has pretty much done away with personal responsibility. We are encouraged to blame our problems on our childhood, our parents, or the wealthy.

Francis preached from the idea that a man's faults were his own, due to his own free will and personal choices.

PRAYER. *All of us must appear before the judgment seat of Christ so that each one may receive suitable recompense.* (2 Cor 5:10)

F OLKS of every age hastened to see and to hear this man for Francis did cast forth demons, heal the sick, and by the might of his preaching did soften hard hearts.

Bonaventure, *The Life of St. Francis*, 12, 8

REFLECTION. Francis' life was a mirror of the Life of Christ, not only in holiness, but also in power.

Jesus' life is our model, as we are to continue the work that Christ began in His time on earth.

PRAYER. *So be imitators of God, as beloved children, and walk in love as Christ loved.*

(Eph 5:1)

T WAS the custom of that angelic man, **APR.**
Francis, never to be slothful in good, but **20**
rather, like the heavenly spirits on Jacob's
ladder, to be ever ascending toward God,
or stooping toward his neighbor.

Bonaventure, *The Life of St. Francis*, 13, 1

REFLECTION. *The Catechism of the Catholic Church* describes the Christian faithful as "always on the way." Our present state is not static, but like a journey—always changing.

If we are not actively striving to grow in holiness we risk sliding back, but we never stand still.

PRAYER. *I press on toward the finish line to win the heavenly prize.* (Phil 3:14)

 E HAD learned to apportion the time **APR.**
granted to him for merit, so that one **21**
part he would spend in laboring for
the profit of his neighbors, the other
he would devote to contemplation.

Bonaventure, *The Life of St. Francis*, 13, 1

REFLECTION. God gave over 600 laws to the Israelites, and He summed them all up in one statement: love God, and love your neighbor.

Francis' life was a constant effort to live this law perfectly.

PRAYER. *You shall love the Lord your God with all your heart. . . . You shall love your neighbor as yourself. Everything . . . depends on these two.* (Mt 22:37-40)

ACCORDINGLY, two years before he yielded his spirit to heaven, the divine counsel leading him, he was brought after many and varied toils to a high mountain apart, that is called Mount Alverno.

APR. 22

Bonaventure, *The Life of St. Francis*, 13, 1

REFLECTION. After years of preaching to large crowds, Francis longed for solitude.

But, as we learn what was to happen to him on Mount Alverno, we will see that his holiness was also increased from his time among men.

PRAYER. *But Jesus often withdrew to lonely places to pray.* (Lk 5:16)

HE WAS filled to overflowing, as never before, with the sweetness of heavenly contemplation, and was kindled with a yet more burning flame of heavenly longings, and began to feel the gifts of the Divine heaped upon him.

APR. 23

Bonaventure, *The Life of St. Francis*, 13, 1

REFLECTION. When you consider how holy Francis was before this experience, we can hardly imagine what it meant that he was filled "as never before."

No matter how much progress we make, God has more waiting for us.

PRAYER. *To him who can do immeasurably more than we could ever ask for or imagine . . . be glory in the Church and in Christ Jesus.* (Eph 3:20)

HE WAS raised to the heights, not like a curious examiner, but even as a faithful and wise servant, searching out the will of God, for it was ever his chief desire to conform himself to it in every way.

Bonaventure, *The Life of St. Francis*, 13, 1

REFLECTION. As Francis begins his mystical experience, he does not enter into it with curiosity. That would put the focus on himself.

Rather, he enters in as a servant, to do the will of God ever more fully. Francis' life shows us what that attitude can accomplish.

PRAYER. *When you have done all that you were ordered, say, "We are unprofitable servants; we have only done our duty."* (Lk 17:10)

———

FRANCIS understood that, as he had imitated Christ in the deeds of his life, so he would be made like Him in the trials and sufferings of His Passion before he should depart from this world.

Bonaventure, *The Life of St. Francis*, 13, 2

REFLECTION. Francis' life followed Jesus' in many ways. It began with the stripping off of his "glory," followed by mortification and temptation by the devil.

Francis had his period of preaching and miracles, and now he would know His Passion.

PRAYER. *Rejoice insofar as you are sharing in the sufferings of Christ.* (1 Pet 4:13)

NE day, close to the Feast of the Holy Cross, while he was praying on the side of the mountain, he beheld a Seraph having six wings, flaming and resplendent, coming down from the heights of heaven.

APR. 26

Bonaventure, *The Life of St. Francis*, 13, 3

REFLECTION. Many Saints have had mystical experiences wherein they were visited by Angels.

When we surrender to God and receive His grace through acts of self-denial, prayer, and the sacraments, we too can experience manifestations of God's Spirit.

PRAYER. *Are not all angels ministering spirits sent forth to serve?*

(Heb 1:14)

HERE appeared between the wings the Figure of a Man crucified, having his hands and feet fastened to a Cross, and he understood that he was to be wholly transformed into the likeness of Christ Crucified.

APR. 27

Bonaventure, *The Life of St. Francis*, 13, 3

REFLECTION. Christ was a hero-figure as He walked the earth preaching and healing.

But to be like Christ in His power, we must share also in His suffering.

PRAYER. *You don't know what you are asking. Can you drink the cup I am going to drink?*

(Mt 20:22)

AS THE vision disappeared, it left in his heart a wondrous glow, and there began to appear in his hands and feet the marks of the nails, even as he had just beheld them in that Figure of the Crucified.

APR. 28

Bonaventure, *The Life of St. Francis*, 13, 3

REFLECTION. There are many Saints who have received the "Stigmata"—the wounds of Christ on their bodies.

Seems odd that total union with Christ should lead to the ultimate suffering. The very thing which by nature we most strongly avoid becomes our reward.

PRAYER. *All I want . . . is to share in his sufferings by becoming conformed to his death.*

(Phil 3:10)

THE right side, moreover, was—as if it had been pierced by a lance—seared with a ruddy scar, where often the sacred blood poured forth, staining his habit and undergarments.

APR. 29

Bonaventure, *The Life of St. Francis*, 13, 3

REFLECTION. Christ had five sacred wounds— His hands and feet were nailed, and a spear pierced His side.

The piercing of the heart of Christ is a powerful image of the fullness of His sacrifice for us.

PRAYER. *But one of the soldiers thrust a lance into his side, and immediately a flow of blood and water came forth.*

(Jn 19:34)

FRANCIS descended from the mountain bearing with him the likeness of the Crucified, graven not on tablets of stone, but written on his flesh by the finger of the Living God.

Bonaventure, *The Life of St. Francis*, 13, 5

APR. 30

REFLECTION. Moses brought God's word to people when he came down from the mountain with the tablets of the law.

Francis came down from the mountain to bring the people Christ, Whose suffering was now written on his flesh.

PRAYER. *When Moses came down from Mount Sinai with the two tablets of the covenant . . . he was not aware that his face was radiant because he had spoken with the* LORD. *(Ex 34:29)*

THE Lord Jesus said to His disciples: "I am the Way, and the Truth, and the Life. No man cometh to the Father, but by Me." Admonitions, 1

MAY 1

REFLECTION. Thus begin the *Admonitions* of St. Francis to his followers. We associate many traits with St. Francis, and these make up what we call "Franciscan." Things like poverty, peace, and love of nature.

But while we might think of all these things as "the Franciscan Way," for Francis there was only one way—Jesus Christ.

PRAYER. *Lord, how can we know the way?*

(Jn 14:5)

HEN you see a poor person, you are looking into a mirror of the Lord and His poor mother.

Celano, *Second Life*, 85

MAY 2

REFLECTION. Christ Himself urged us to see Him in the poor in the parable of the sheep and goats.

All the great Saints took this directive very seriously. One Saint even used to ask the poor for their blessings.

PRAYER. *Lord, when did we see you hungry and give you something to eat, or thirsty and give you something to drink?* (Mt 25:37)

HE Lord was pleased to confirm the teaching of St. Francis, not only by miraculous signs, but also by the marks of his stigmata, so that no believer could question them on external evidence.

From a Sermon of St. Bonaventure, October 4, 1255

MAY 3

REFLECTION. People will always doubt miracles. Even with proof, skepticism remains.

But when there is selfless service to the poor, such as with St. Francis or Mother Teresa, the secular world shows respect and admiration almost equal to that of the believers.

PRAYER. *This is how everyone will know that you are my disciples: if you love one another.* (Jn 13:35)

FRANCIS said, if our hearts are on fire with longing for our heavenly home, we will have no trouble enduring the outer cold. **MAY 4**

Bonaventure, *Major Life*, 5:2

REFLECTION. How time consuming, how distracting, is our constant concern for personal comforts!

How much time do we spend making sure we are not too hot, or too cold, not the least bit hungry, or thirsty? Francis did not worry about these things, but focused all his time and effort on serving God.

PRAYER. *And so I say to you, do not be anxious about your life.*

(Mt 6:25)

 FRANCIS wished that everything should sing pilgrimage and exile. **MAY 5**

Celano, *Second Life*, 60

REFLECTION. When people know that the end is near, they experience a strange liberation. Whether it's the last day on the job, the day before vacation, or senior year of high school. Suddenly, everything feels different—less stressful. You wonder what you had been so uptight about before.

Christians who grasp that life is short and finite can experience this freedom that Francis wished for all his brothers.

PRAYER. *The city we now live in will not last.*

(Heb 13:14)

SERVANT of God is a picture of God, in which God is honored for His favor. *Mirror of Perfection,* 45

REFLECTION. Every human is made in the image of God. But when the world encounters a true Saint, such as Francis of Assisi, they see God more clearly reflected in that person.

This is why Saints deserve our veneration, not for their individual person, but for the way in which they model what humanity is capable of.

PRAYER. *We hold this treasure in jars of clay.* (2 Cor 4:7)

 ND you may not claim credit that God is pictured through you, for compared to Him you are less than the wood and paint.

Mirror of Perfection, 45

REFLECTION. When we go to the museum we may admire the paintings and think them very beautiful, but we don't honor the canvas and the paint; we honor the artist who fashioned the elements into a beautiful work.

That same canvas and dye could have easily been made into a potato sack. It's not the materials, but the artist.

PRAYER. *For we are God's handiwork, created in Christ Jesus for a life of good works.* (Eph 2:10)

HE Rule and life of these brothers is this: namely, to live in obedience and chastity, and without property, and to follow the doctrine and footsteps of our Lord Jesus Christ.

MAY 8

The Rule of the Friars Minor, 1

REFLECTION. Franciscans, like all religious men and women, take vows of poverty, chastity, and obedience.

Why these three, out of all the other virtues? It speaks of the danger posed to our spiritual life by their opposites: affluence, impurity, and selfishness.

PRAYER. *Anyone who wishes to follow me must deny himself, take up his cross, and follow me.* (Mt 16:24)

HE year of probation being finished, let him be received to obedience. Afterwards it shall not be lawful for him to pass to another Order, nor to "wander about beyond obedience."

MAY 9

The Rule of the Friars Minor, 2

REFLECTION. Francis expected his friars to spend their lives in one place under simple obedience.

How easy it is to keep one's options open, to try something new. We consider this being true to one's self. However, it may just be an inability to be true to anyone else.

PRAYER. *No one who puts his hand on the plow, and then looks back, is ready for the reign of God.* (Lk 9:62)

BUT the other brothers who have promised obedience may have one tunic with a hood, and another without a hood, if necessity require it, and a cord and breeches. **MAY 10** The Rule of the Friars Minor, 2

REFLECTION. Have you ever been late because you couldn't figure out what to wear? Have you ever been self-conscious about what you were wearing?

The Franciscan focus on poverty does more than humble the friar, it frees him from the chains of his own self-absorption.

PRAYER. *And why are you so concerned about your clothing?* (Mt 6:28)

AND although they should be called hypocrites, let them not cease to do good. **MAY 11** The Rule of the Friars Minor, 2

REFLECTION. The Franciscan rule proposes a rigorous and demanding life of exceptional holiness.

Father Francis knew that his friars would fail, and their failure would be called out as hypocrisy. But he made clear that this inevitable failure was not to become an excuse for giving up in their efforts to be holy.

PRAYER. *Neither will I condemn you. Go on your way, and sin no more.* (Jn 8:11)

THE clerics shall say the Office, and say it for the living and the dead; but to satisfy for the defect and negligence of the brothers, let them say every day Psalm 51 with the Our Father. **MAY 12** The Rule of the Friars Minor, 3

REFLECTION. Daily penance and praying for the dead are deeply Catholic practices, yet how far have they fallen out of favor!

At the very least, we ask for forgiveness and pray for the dead each Sunday at Mass.

PRAYER. *Wash me completely from my guilt and cleanse me from my sin.* (Ps 51:4)

AND all the brothers shall likewise fast from the feast of All Saints until the Nativity of our Lord, and from Epiphany, when our Lord Jesus Christ began to fast, until Easter. **MAY 13** The Rule of the Friars Minor, 3

REFLECTION. The Church's liturgical calendar has changed since Francis' day, but the periods he refers to would be like our Advent and Lent.

While most Catholics (and nearly everyone else) celebrate Christmas and Easter with joy and over-indulgence, it is Franciscan to also observe the subdued self-restraint of Advent and Lent.

PRAYER. *A time to weep, a time to laugh, a time to mourn, and a time to dance.* (Eccl 3:4)

ET all the brothers who are appointed ministers and servants of the other brothers place them where they may be, and let them often visit and spiritually admonish and console them.

The Rule of the Friars Minor, 4

MAY
14

REFLECTION. We are all appointed to minister to and serve certain people in our lives.

Let us remember to visit them often, to spiritually admonish them when necessary, and console them at all times.

PRAYER. *When did we see you ill or in prison and come to visit you?*

(Mt 25:39)

O THEM is committed the care of the souls of their brothers. If any should be lost through their fault and bad example, they will have to give an account before the Lord Jesus Christ in the day of judgment.

The Rule of the Friars Minor, 5

MAY
15

REFLECTION. Franciscan leaders are servant leaders, and yet, that does not excuse them from accountability for their faults or bad example.

To lead like Francis means to hold oneself to a high standard.

PRAYER. *Tend carefully to yourself and to the whole flock, wherein the Holy Spirit has placed you.*

(Acts 20:28)

ND let all the brothers take care not **MAY** to be troubled or angered because of the fault or bad example of another, for the devil desires to corrupt many through the sin of one.

The Rule of the Friars Minor, 5

REFLECTION. Paying attention to sin has the unfortunate effect of magnifying it. As if the devil uses each sin as a promotional campaign for the next one.

It is not only the imitation of the sin that he is after. He'll settle for pride, gossip, and slander.

PRAYER. *I urge you to avoid those who cause dissension and offenses contrary to what you have learned. Avoid them.* (Rom 16:17)

 ND let the brothers who know how **MAY** to work labor in that art they understand and they can exercise it becomingly. And let every man abide in the art or employment wherein he was called. The Rule of the Friars Minor, 7

17

REFLECTION. When we think of holy men, we think of their prayer life, but the Franciscan is also called to work, as are all Christians.

The biblical record is clear on this—all Christians must be hard working, steady, and faithful in their jobs.

PRAYER. *Make it your aim to do the work of your hands quietly, focused on the task which is given to you.* (1 Thes 4:11)

77

AND let them take care not to appear exteriorly sad and gloomy like hypocrites, but let them show themselves to be joyful and contented in the Lord, merry and courteous.

MAY
18

The Rule of the Friars Minor, 7

REFLECTION. If it's been said that happiness is a kind of courage, then joy is a kind of faith.

Indeed joy is considered to be the mark of a true Christian, for it reveals an understanding of the situation, whatever it may be—God is in control, and God is good.

PRAYER. *Rejoice in the Lord always. Again, I say, rejoice!*

(Phil 4:4)

FOR we ought not to have more use and esteem of money and coins than of stones. If we should chance to find money in any place, let us no more regard it than the dust we tread under our feet.

MAY
19

The Rule of the Friars Minor, 8

REFLECTION. This complete disregard for money and possessions is hard to grasp—and hard to practice—in our consumer society.

But renouncing all possessions was the first and most dramatic act of Francis' conversion. If we miss this, we may miss the Franciscan way entirely.

PRAYER. *To be content with holiness is to profit greatly.*

(1 Tim 6:6)

ND they ought to rejoice when they converse with mean and despised persons, with the poor and the weak, and with those who beg in the streets. **MAY 20** The Rule of the Friars Minor, 9

REFLECTION. As with disregard for money, the idea of being happy to associate with street people, the deformed, the sick—this is hard! Too often our forms of helping the poor are done remotely. We don't have a chance to look them in the eye, interact with them, or touch them.

Direct contact with the poor was just one more way that Francis managed to live out the Gospel in a literal fashion.

PRAYER. *When you host a gathering, invite the poor, the crippled, the lame and the blind.*

(Lk 14:13)

 ET one make known clearly his wants to another, in order that he may receive what is necessary for him. And let everyone love and nourish his brother as a mother loves, so far as God gives them grace. **MAY 21** The Rule of the Friars Minor, 9

REFLECTION. In the midst of all this renunciation and self-denial, Francis knew that the brothers would need to rely on each other for support and to get their needs met.

This interdependence is the natural functioning of the Body of Christ.

PRAYER. *And all the believers stuck together, and shared with each other.* *(Acts 2:44)*

ASK the sick brother that he give thanks to the Creator for all things, and that he desire to be as God wills him to be; for all are disciplined by the rod of afflictions and infirmities. **MAY 22** The Rule of the Friars Minor, 10

REFLECTION. One never thinks of Francis as someone who was unhappy, yet he embraced everything we avoid.

In this section of the Rule, Francis urges his brothers to rejoice and praise God in their hardships, and to see in their illness God's loving hand.

PRAYER. *Rejoice always. Never stop praying. Constantly give thanks.* *(1 Thes 5:16-18)*

 ND let all the brothers take care not to calumniate anyone, nor to contend in words; let them indeed study to maintain silence as far as God gives them grace. **MAY 23** The Rule of the Friars Minor, 11

REFLECTION. Speaking is a risky activity.

We don't think of the risk each time we open our mouth, like we do each time we step onto an airplane, but all know the danger and the damage of words.

PRAYER. *In a multitude of words there is no lack of sin, but the one who keeps silence is most wise.* *(Prov 10:19)*

ENJOIN all the brothers that when they travel through the world they in no way have any beast of burden. Nor to ride on horseback unless they are compelled by infirmity or great necessity.

MAY 24

The Rule of the Friars Minor, 15

REFLECTION. It is almost as if Father Francis wanted the brothers to have a handicap, to accomplish their work without money, wardrobe, and transportation.

The net effect of course, was to put the friar's reliance on God rather than on any created thing.

PRAYER. *As he sent them out to preach the kingdom of God and heal the sick, he said, "Take nothing for your journey."* (Lk 9:2-3)

 BESEECH that my brothers glory not, nor rejoice on account of good works which God may sometimes operate in them. Let us know for certain that nothing belongs to us but vices and sins.

MAY 25

The Rule of the Friars Minor, 17

REFLECTION. Of all the things a Franciscan is called to renounce, perhaps nothing is more difficult than renouncing one's own self.

Pride, ego, selfishness, all these things cling to us more tenaciously than money, clothes, or possessions ever could.

PRAYER. *Let go of your old self which is corrupted by its own erroneous desires.* (Eph 4:22)

LET all the brothers be Catholics, and live and speak in a Catholic manner. But if anyone should err from the Catholic faith, and will not amend, let him be expelled. **MAY 26**

The Rule of the Friars Minor, 19

REFLECTION. The values of St. Francis, especially his love and care for creation are very popular in the 21st century with Christians and non-Christians alike.

Francis did not hold any of his values in isolation. All were part of the Catholic Christian doctrine which gave them both context and balance.

PRAYER. *I am content as long as the gospel is preached, whether it be sincere or opportunistic.* *(Phil 1:18)*

THOSE who unjustly inflict upon us tribulation, shame, injuries, sorrows, martyrdom and death are our friends whom we ought to love much, because we gain eternal life by what they make us suffer. **MAY 27**

The Rule of the Friars Minor, 22

REFLECTION. Loving our enemies seems so difficult and hardly worth the effort.

Francis suggests that, through the suffering they cause us, our enemies help us get to heaven. For that, we should thank them, and see them as God's instruments for our good.

PRAYER. *Love your enemies, and your reward shall be great.* *(Lk 6:35)*

82

UT now, after having renounced the **MAY** world, we have nothing else to do but to be solicitous, to follow the will of God, and to please Him.

28

The Rule of the Friars Minor, 22

REFLECTION. We live in an age of options. Whether it's a soft drink, a home or a career, there are too many possibilities.

This is the beauty of the complete renunciation of the Franciscans—all the options are gone. Bridges burned, exits sealed—all that's left is to serve God completely.

PRAYER. *When you come to serve the Lord, stand firm and be sincere.* (Sir 2:1)

 ND let us be much on our guard **MAY** against the malice and cunning of Satan, who going about seeks to seduce the heart under pretext of some reward.

29

The Rule of the Friars Minor, 22

REFLECTION. Our biggest enemy may be our own ego and selfish desires.

But the entire biblical record, and especially Jesus Himself, speaks of a malicious, external force outside of us who is focused on our destruction.

PRAYER. *Satan desires to have you that he might sift you like wheat.* (Lk 22:31)

ET us love with all our heart, soul, mind, with all our strength and understanding the Lord God Who has created and redeemed us, and by His mercy will save us. **MAY 30** *The Rule of the Friars Minor, 23*

REFLECTION. As the Rule draws to a close, Francis reminds his brothers of the greatest of all commandments and the foundational principle that runs the entire length of the Bible.

PRAYER. *You shall love the Lord your God with your whole heart and with your whole soul and with your whole mind and with your whole strength. This is the first commandment.*

(Mk 12:30)

ESIRE nothing else, wish for nothing else except our Creator and Redeemer, and Savior, the only true God, Who is full of good, all good, the true and supreme good, Who alone is good. **MAY 31** *The Rule of the Friars Minor, 23*

REFLECTION. So much about the Franciscan way is helpful to our lives in this world, and indeed good for creation itself.

And yet, for Francis, the goal of the entire Franciscan way was to delight in God, the one true good above all things this world can offer.

PRAYER. *My soul thirsts for God, the living God.* (Ps 42:3)

BECAUSE God is a spirit, therefore it is only by the spirit He can be seen, for "it is the spirit that gives life; the flesh profits nothing." **JUNE 1**

Admonitions, 1

REFLECTION. Francis gives his followers the message that sanctity is a work of the Holy Spirit.

While most of the things we seek in life depend on our own hard work and rugged individualism, that is not the way with achieving holiness. Only a movement of the Holy Spirit can make us holy.

PRAYER. *It is the spirit that gives life; the flesh can achieve nothing.*

(Jn 6:63)

FROM His "royal throne" He came into the womb of the Virgin; daily He descends from the bosom of His Father upon the altar in the hands of the priest. **JUNE 2**

Admonitions, 1

REFLECTION. Though not all may achieve the sanctity of seeing God in the spirit, God is still no less accessible to us.

He humbles himself daily to come to us under the appearance of bread in Holy Communion.

PRAYER. *Whoever feeds upon my flesh and drinks my blood has eternal life.*

(Jn 6:54)

S HE appeared in true flesh to the Apostles, so now He shows Himself to us in the sacred Bread. In this way our Lord is ever with His faithful, as He says: "Behold I am with you always." **JUNE 3**

Admonitions, 1

REFLECTION. In the Eucharist, Christ makes it possible for His followers to experience Him in the flesh.

This is perhaps even more intimate than what those who walked with Him on earth knew.

PRAYER. *Whoever feeds upon my flesh and drinks my blood dwells in me and I dwell in him.* (Jn 6:56)

DAM might eat of every tree of paradise and so long as he did not offend against obedience he did not sin. **JUNE 4**

Admonitions, 2

REFLECTION. Evil is a sort of overreaching. When we fail to appreciate all the goods we have and focus only on the few we do not have, the evil of self-will appears.

Francis knew this, because even in his poverty, he recognized that God gives everyone everything he or she needs to live and to serve Him.

PRAYER. *His divine power has given us everything we need for life and for holiness through our knowledge of him.* (2 Pet 1:3)

F AT times a subject sees things which **JUNE**
would be better or more useful than those
which his superior commands, let him sacrifice his will to God, and strive to fulfill
the work enjoined by the superior.

5

Admonitions, 3

REFLECTION. Surely we would all obey a command from God Himself, but what about our
boss, or spouse, or neighbor?

Obedience is much more than doing what we
have to do. Obedience starts with putting what
others need ahead of our own desires.

PRAYER. *Be subject to one another out of reverence for Christ.*

(Eph 5:21)

OR there are many religious who, under **JUNE**
pretext of seeing better things than those
which their superiors command, look
back and return to the vomit of their
own will.

6

Admonitions, 3

REFLECTION. When we obey because we agree
with the request, or think our superiors wiser
than we are, we do not experience the benefits
of true obedience.

The virtue of obedience comes from over-
coming our own ego and self-will. Its fruit is humility.

PRAYER. *Those with a wise heart are willing to
take orders.*

(Prov 10:8)

ET those who are set above others glory in this superiority only as much as if they had been deputed to wash the feet of the brothers. **JUNE 7** Admonitions, 4

REFLECTION. Leadership, management and authority require people that can be lead, managed and overseen. Without followers, there can be no leaders.

This makes those under authority the most essential part of the equation.

PRAYER. *Those considered to be rulers among the Gentiles lord it over them and their great ones make their authority over them felt. But this must not be so with you.* (Mk 10:42-43)

 ONSIDER, O man, how great the excellence in which the Lord has placed you because He has created and formed you to the image of His beloved Son according to His own likeness. **JUNE 8** Admonitions, 5

REFLECTION. In the creation account God goes about His work pretty methodically, until He reaches the creation of man.

Then, God pauses, reflects, and does something completely different. Only man is created in God's own image.

PRAYER. *And God said, "Let us make man in our own image, to be like us and to rule over everything that moves upon the earth."* (Gen 1:26)

F YOU were so clever and wise that you **JUNE** possessed all knowledge, you could not glory in all this, because one demon has **9** known more of heavenly things and still knows more of earthly things than all men.

Admonitions, 5

REFLECTION. What we think or believe is helpful to the Christian when such thoughts lead to right actions.

Actions are a true measure of holiness.

PRAYER. *So you believe that God exists. Good for you. The devil also believes in God, and he shudders at the thought!*

(Jas 2:19)

R IF you were handsome and rich **JUNE** and if you could work wonders and put demons to flight, you could not **10** glory in them. What we may glory in is our infirmities, and in bearing daily the Cross of our Lord Jesus Christ.

Admonitions, 5

REFLECTION. Things we tend to desire—money, ability, power, are generally not praised in the Bible.

Things we tend to run from, like patience, suffering, and humility, are much more prominent.

PRAYER. *Blessed are the meek; blessed are the merciful, blessed are those who are persecuted.*

(Mt 5:5, 7, 10)

LET us all, brothers, consider the Good Shepherd Who to save His sheep bore the suffering of the Cross.

JUNE 11

Admonitions, 6

REFLECTION. How much is enough pain and suffering to bear on behalf of another?

Perhaps Jesus bore the maximum possible pain and suffering to give us an answer to this question.

PRAYER. *In your struggle against sin, you have not yet resisted to the point of shedding your blood.* (Heb 12:4)

 WHEREFORE it is a great shame for us, the servants of God, that, whereas the Saints have practiced works, we should expect to receive honor and glory for merely reading and preaching them.

JUNE 12

Admonitions, 6

REFLECTION. Let us avoid the trap of believing that by merely thinking or publishing an idea we have made a difference.

Let us give thanks to God when what we speak or write inspires right action.

PRAYER. *Who among you is wise and understanding? Prove by your good life that your works are done with the humility that comes from wisdom.* (Jas 3:13)

WHOEVER, therefore, envies his brother on account of the good which the Lord says or does in him, commits a sin akin to blasphemy, because he envies the Most High Himself who says and does all that is good. Admonitions, 8

JUNE 13

REFLECTION. The desire to be the center of attention, to be better than others, to be loved and appreciated seems to set us on the wrong road from the very beginning.

Giving all glory to God is the better bet. You can never go wrong there.

PRAYER. *All good giving and all the best gifts come from above, coming down from the Father of light.*
(Jas 1:17)

HE TRULY loves his enemy who does not grieve because of the wrong done to himself, but who is afflicted for love of God because of the sin on his brother's soul. Admonitions, 9

JUNE 14

REFLECTION. True love is more concerned with the beloved than with the self. True love does not wonder, "What can she do for me?" but rather, "How can I help her?"

Christian love strives to do this for everyone, even our enemies.

PRAYER. *Love is not obnoxious, does not put its own needs first, and does not get angry or think bad of another.*
(1 Cor 13:5)

HERE are many who if they commit sin **JUNE 15** or suffer wrong often blame their enemy or their neighbor. But this is not right, for each one has his enemy in his power,—to wit, the body by which he sins. Admonitions, 10

REFLECTION. All the great spiritual writers have two things in common.

First, they insist on personal responsibility for one's actions, and secondly, they slowly remove all excuses until one is left to face the fact that our faults are indeed in ourselves.

PRAYER. *God tempts no one. Rather, temptation occurs when someone is attracted and seduced by his own desire.* (Jas 1:13-14)

O THE servant of God, nothing **JUNE 16** should be displeasing save sin. Admonitions, 11

REFLECTION. In the midst of all of the strictness of St. Francis' admonitions comes this beautiful reminder that there is a liberation that comes from the renunciation of sin and all its trappings.

Truly the one who loses his life for the sake of the Gospel will find it.

PRAYER. *For everything created by God is good, and nothing is to be rejected, provided it is received with thanksgiving.* (1 Tim 4:4)

THE servant of God who does not trouble himself or get angry about anything lives uprightly and without sin.

JUNE 17

Admonitions, 11

REFLECTION. You may want to read that again. How does one live without sin? By maintaining one's own inner peace.

Finding the self-control to maintain peace at all times is not easy, but surely requires keeping our focus on God.

PRAYER. *You will keep in perfect peace, those whose mind is fixed on you, for they trust in you.*

(Isa 26:3)

AND blessed is he who keeps nothing for himself, rendering "to Cæsar the things that are Cæsar's and to God the things that are God's." Admonitions, 11

JUNE 18

REFLECTION. Paintings or statues of St. Francis often show him with his hands outstretched looking up to the heavens. Never clutching, never focused inward, but always outward.

The hands give back to the world what is worldly, and the upturned face gives to God what is God's.

PRAYER. *Jesus said, "You need to do just one more thing: sell everything you have and give the money to the poor."*

(Lk 18:22)

THUS may the servant of God know if he has the Spirit of God: if when the Lord works some good through him, his body is not therefore puffed up; and if he esteems himself less than other men. *Admonitions, 12*

REFLECTION. The amazing power of the Holy Spirit at work in us is able to neutralize our ego, and dispel our pride. This allows us to manifest our true self.

In this way God teaches us that we can only truly be ourselves, when by the power of His Holy Spirit, we cease focusing on ourselves.

PRAYER. *The fruit of the spirit is love, joy and peace . . . .* (Gal 5:22)

HOW much interior patience and humility a servant of God may have cannot be known so long as he is contented, but only when those who ought to please him go against him. *Admonitions, 13*

REFLECTION. Grace under pressure is rare. And patience does not come naturally, especially when we are not getting our way.

Only through the supernatural power of the Holy Spirit can we keep our patience when things get stressful.

PRAYER. *The fruit of the spirit is . . . patience, kindness, gentleness and self-control.* (Gal 5:22-23)

ANY apply themselves to prayers and practice much abstinence and bodily mortification, but because of a single word or because of something being taken from them, they are scandalized and troubled.

Admonitions, 14

REFLECTION. Think about it as getting a return on an investment.

For all the hours we invest in prayer, spiritual reading, at Mass and parish activities, shouldn't we get a return of virtue when we are tempted, or peace when we are troubled?

PRAYER. *Blessed is the man who fears the Lord, he has no fear of bad news.* (Ps 112:1, 7)

 HEY are truly peacemakers who amidst all they suffer in this world maintain peace in soul and body for the love of our Lord Jesus Christ. Admonitions, 15

REFLECTION. When you come to the point where you know that suffering is part of life, and you expect it, and you embrace it for the love of Jesus Christ, then you have nothing to fear.

You have conquered the world.

PRAYER. *Those who sow the seeds of peace, and cultivate peace, bear the fruit of righteousness.* (Jas 3:18)

HEY are clean of heart who despise earthly things and always seek those of heaven, and who never cease to adore and contemplate the Lord God, Living and True, with a pure heart and mind. **JUNE 23** Admonitions, 16

REFLECTION. If we can withdraw our attention from all the stimulation that surrounds us every moment of every day to just think on the Lord, and contemplate Him, this will purify our hearts.

PRAYER. *And as we gaze upon the glory of the Lord with unveiled faces, all of us are being transformed into that same image, from glory to glory.* (2 Cor 3:18)

 LESSED is that servant who is not more puffed up because of the good the Lord says and works through him than because of that which He says and works through others. **JUNE 24** Admonitions, 17

REFLECTION. Pride is so pernicious that it even shows up in those who are trying to serve the Lord well.

It doesn't take long before a genuine life of humble service to the Lord becomes a cult of personality around the minister.

PRAYER. *Many will say to me on that day, "Lord, did we not cast out demons in your name?" And I will tell them plainly, "I never knew you."* (Mt 7:22-23)

LESSED is the man who bears with his neighbor according to the frailty of his nature as much as he would wish to be borne with by him if he should be in a like case. **JUNE 25** Admonitions, 18

REFLECTION. The Golden Rule is so basic, so logical, so easy to agree with, yet so utterly difficult to practice!

One way to start is to simply put ourselves in the other's shoes, to practice empathy and sympathy. Practice is really the operative word, for empathy does require practice. It takes many intentional efforts before we can make it a habit.

PRAYER. *In everything, deal with others as you would like them to deal with you.* (Mt 7:12)

LESSED is the servant who does not regard himself as better when he is esteemed by men than when he is reputed as mean and despicable: for what a man is in the sight of God, so much he is, and no more. **JUNE 26** Admonitions, 20

REFLECTION. It is unavoidable that our own opinion of ourselves is tied to what others think of us.

But the actual state of someone's soul as it is known to God is something that only He knows.

PRAYER. *O Lord, you have examined me, and you know me.* (Ps 139:1)

LESSED is that servant who does not **JUNE** speak through hope of reward and who does not manifest everything and is not **27** "hasty to speak," but who wisely foresees what he ought to say and answer.

Admonitions, 22

REFLECTION. Each time we speak, we do so for some purpose. Most often, words are driven by ego—to get noticed, to defend, to prove a point, and so on.

The first step in making our speech virtuous is to pause and think before we speak.

PRAYER. *Everyone should be quick to listen but slow to speak and slow to anger.* (Jas 1:19)

LESSED is the servant who bears disci- **JUNE** pline, accusation, and blame from oth- ers as patiently as if they came from **28** himself.

Admonitions, 23

REFLECTION. St. Francis lived almost a millennium before the advent of modern psychology, but his admonitions show a clear understanding of the human ego, and the necessity of fighting to master our inordinate love of self.

PRAYER. *What is the source of these conflicts and quarrels among you? Are they not the result of your passions that are at war within you?* (Jas 4:1)

BLESSED is the servant who mildly submits, modestly obeys, humbly confesses, and willingly satisfies. Who does not make excuses and who humbly bears shame and rebuke when he is without fault. **JUNE 29**   Admonitions, 23

REFLECTION. Our ego wants to protect our self-image from any contradiction or insult. Our ego wants to "save" our life.

But Jesus makes it clear that we must "lose" our life, by letting go instead of holding on to our self-love.

PRAYER. *If someone is suing you for the shirt off your back, give him your coat to go with it.*

(Mt 5:40)

 BY THIS I wish to know if thou lovest God, to wit: that there be no brother in the world who has sinned, however great his sin may be, who after he has seen Thy face shall ever go away without Thy mercy. **JUNE 30**   To a Certain Minister

REFLECTION. When the inevitable challenges come, we are required to meet these offenses with mercy and forgiveness.

The constant remembrance of how much God has forgiven us should make this required mercy much easier to practice.

PRAYER. *You must forgive, just as the Lord has forgiven you.*

(Col 3:13b)

BESEECH Thee, O Lord, that the fiery and **JULY**
sweet strength of Thy love may absorb my
soul from all things that are under heaven, **1**
that I may die for love of Thy love as Thou
did deign to die for love of my love.

Prayer to Obtain Divine Love

REFLECTION. Like all the great mystic Saints, Francis had a glimpse of the fullness of God and what it meant to truly enter into His love.

Words fail when mystics gain this intimate knowledge of God's love.

PRAYER. *May you know Christ's love, which is beyond knowledge, that you may be filled with the fullness of God.* (Eph 3:19)

 HOU art holy, Lord God, Who alone **JULY**
works wonders. Thou art strong. Thou
art great. Thou art most high. Thou **2**
art the Almighty King, Thou, Holy Father, King of heaven and earth.

The Praises of God

REFLECTION. With the amazing amount of security, ease, and comfort we enjoy in developed countries, there is less and less need for physical strength in our lives. We are less threatened, less in need of a strong protector.

Most of our threats are now psychological, emotional, and financial. God's power and strength are there for us in these ways as well.

PRAYER. *The Lord is my strength and my shield; my heart places its trust in him.* (Ps 28:7)

100

HOU art the Lord God Triune and One; all good. Thou art good, all good, highest good, Lord God living and true. Thou art charity, love. Thou art wisdom.

The Praises of God

REFLECTION. What does it mean to be good? This is not something people talk about—or agree on much these days.

As we come to know God's goodness through His acts recorded in the Bible, we see His faithfulness, protection, love, long suffering, and His justice, and we begin to understand what it means to be good.

PRAYER. *Jesus said, "Why do you call me good? No one is good but God alone."* (Mk 10:18)

HOU art humility. Thou art patience. Thou art quietude. Thou art joy and gladness. Thou art justice and temperance.

The Praises of God

REFLECTION. These praises show God's restraint, His peace and quiet, temperance. It is hard to think of God as still and small, but that is certainly part of Who God is.

God is not always in the storm. Sometimes, He is in the whisper.

PRAYER. *After the earthquake there came a fire, but God was not in the fire either. Then came a still small voice. When Elijah heard it he hid his face in his cloak.* (1 Ki 19:12-13)

THOU art beauty. Thou art meekness. Thou art protector. Thou art guardian and defender. Thou art strength. Thou art refreshment. The Praises of God

REFLECTION. Refreshment, strength, beauty, even protection—all describe the Sabbath rest that God has given us. There is a power in being able to rest, be at peace, and refresh one's self.

The detail of God's resting on the seventh day of creation is one of God's greatest gifts to us.

PRAYER. *Six days you shall do your work, but the seventh day you shall rest and keep Sabbath, that you and all that is yours may be refreshed.* (Ex 23:12)

 THOU art our hope. Thou art our faith. Thou art our great sweetness. Thou art our eternal life, great and admirable Lord, God Almighty, merciful Savior. The Praises of God

REFLECTION. In a world where almost everything we eat is filled with sugar, it is hard to appreciate the blessing of sweetness. We glimpse it occasionally in a perfect strawberry or peach.

God's sweetness comes through in His word and in the comfort of the Bible.

PRAYER. *Your words are sweet to my taste; sweeter than honey in my mouth.* (Ps 119:103)

AY the Lord bless thee and keep thee. May He show His face to thee and have mercy on thee. May He turn His countenance to thee and give thee peace. Brother Leo may the Lord bless thee.

JULY 7

The Blessing of Brother Leo

REFLECTION. This very famous "Irish" blessing first appears in the Old Testament.

It touches on so many important things that we want for those we love: ease, safety, mercy, and peace among other things.

PRAYER. *May the Lord bless you and take care of you! May the Lord be kind and gracious to you! May the Lord look on you with favor and give you peace!* (Num 6:24-26)

OST high, omnipotent, good Lord. Praise, glory and honor and benediction all, are Thine. To Thee alone do they belong, most High. There is no man fit to mention Thee.

JULY 8

Canticle of the Sun

REFLECTION. The view from a rooftop, high-rise building or on a mountain is something that always makes us stop and ponder. There is a unique and arresting perspective that comes from being high up.

The Bible often speaks of God as being "on high" as if to suggest that God's perspective is greater than ours.

PRAYER. *Glory to God in the highest heaven.*

(Lk 2:14)

PRAISED be to Thee, my Lord, with all Thy creatures, especially to my worshipful brother sun, which lights up the day, and beautiful is he and radiant with splendor great. *Canticle of the Sun*

REFLECTION. The sun is up in the heavens; it gives us light and heat. Its brightness is inapproachable. Its power is awesome and hard to comprehend. Without it we would not survive.

The many ways that the sun mirrors the attributes of God helps us to understand God's greatness and power.

PRAYER. *O God, be gracious to us and bless us, and let your face shed its light upon us.* (Ps 67:2)

 PRAISED be my Lord, for sister moon and for the stars, in heaven Thou hast formed them clear and precious and fair. *Canticle of the Sun*

REFLECTION. The night sky, like so many of the elements of nature, can be hard for us to totally appreciate.

But even a few experiences of the night sky in all its glory, the amazing grandeur of space and the universe, does indeed prompt one to feel rather small and insignificant.

PRAYER. *When I consider the heavens, the moon and the stars that you have set in place, what is man that you are mindful of him?* (Ps 8:4)

PRAISED be my Lord for brother wind and for the air and clouds and every kind of weather, by which Thou gives to Thy creatures nourishment.

JULY 11

Canticle of the Sun

REFLECTION. God's ways are written in the world around us.

For those who have ears to hear and eyes to see, there is much to be learned about God from nature.

PRAYER. *For as the rain and the snow come down from heaven and water the earth, making it bring forth and blossom, so my word which goes out to the earth does not return to me without bearing fruit.* (Isa 55:10-11)

 PRAISED be my Lord for sister water, which is greatly helpful and humble and precious and pure.

JULY 12

Canticle of the Sun

REFLECTION. If nature teaches us about God, then what can we say about water? It is so versatile, yet so plain; so essential, yet so common, so necessary for life, yet so taken for granted.

A study of water in the Bible reveals how essential it is to God's plan, from the Red Sea to the Jordan and so many places in between.

PRAYER. *But whoever drinks the water that I will give him will never be thirsty; but the water that I give will become a spring of water welling up into eternal life.* (Jn 4:14)

RAISED be my Lord for brother fire, by which Thou lightest up the dark. And fair is he and joyful and mighty and strong. **JULY 13**

Canticle of the Sun

REFLECTION. What does fire teach us about God? That He loves us, certainly, and wants us to be comfortable and full of life.

All these gifts of nature give us language to talk about and understand God.

PRAYER. *Therefore, since we are receiving a kingdom that cannot be shaken, let us be thankful, and so worship God acceptably with reverence and awe, for our "God is a consuming fire."* (Heb 28:29)

 RAISED be my Lord for our sister, mother earth, which sustains and keeps us, and brings forth diverse fruits with grass and flowers bright. **JULY 14**

Canticle of the Sun

REFLECTION. What can be more amazing than a seed growing? While we can explain what happens, can anyone really say how an entire plant is contained inside of that tiny seed?

It is amazing that anyone has a hard time believing in a loving God when the signs that prove His existence are all around us.

PRAYER. *For the earth has yielded its fruit. God, our God, has blessed us. May God still give us his blessings until the ends of the earth revere him.* (Ps 67:7-8)

PRAISED be my Lord for those who for-give on account of Thy love, and endure weakness and trials. Blessed are those who shall endure in peace, for by Thee, most High, they shall be crowned.

JULY 15

Canticle of the Sun

REFLECTION. In the Beatitudes, the blessings for the persecuted and the peacemakers go hand in hand.

Those who seek to make peace will always be persecuted. The challenge is for them to hold on to their own peace and not to lose their focus on what they have set out to do.

PRAYER. *Blessed are the peacemakers. Blessed are those who are persecuted in the cause of justice.*

(Mt 5:9-10)

PRAISED be my Lord for our sister, bodily death, from which no living man can flee. Woe to them who die in mortal sin; blessed are those who shall find them-selves in Thy most holy will.

JULY 16

Canticle of the Sun

REFLECTION. The lifelong struggle to be a peacemaker and to keep oneself in peace, ulti-mately ends in death.

In death, those who have been faithful can experience the peace that we only glimpse tem-porarily on earth.

PRAYER. *These are the ones who have survived the great tribulation. They have washed their robes and made them white in the blood of the Lamb.*

(Rev 7:14)

PRAISE You and bless You my Lord, and give Him thanks, and be subject unto Him with great humility.

Canticle of the Sun

REFLECTION. The praise of God's creation, and the love of "things" should always come back to, end, and be fulfilled in God Himself, Who made all things.

The creation should be loved for the creator.

PRAYER. *Yours O Lord, is the greatness and the power, and the glory and the majesty and the splendor. You are the ruler of all things.*

(1 Chr 29:11)

 LORD, make me an instrument of Your peace.

Make Me an Instrument of Your Peace

REFLECTION. While this prayer was not written by St. Francis, it is widely agreed that it accurately reflects the essence of the Franciscan charism.

To be an instrument of God's peace means to be filled with the Holy Spirit.

PRAYER. *Those who are led by the Spirit of God are children of God. For you did not receive a spirit of slavery leading to fear; rather, you received the Spirit of adoption, enabling us to cry out, Abba! Father!*

(Rom 8:14-15)

N THAT place where there is hate, may I bring love.
Make Me an Instrument of Your Peace

REFLECTION. Love is the ultimate answer to any question about how one should act.

To bring love where there is hate is to bring right thinking where it is wrong. It may not be accepted, but it is still right, because love can do no harm.

PRAYER. *Love cannot result in any harm to the neighbor; therefore, love is the fulfillment of the Law.* (Rom 13:10)

 N THAT place where an offense has been given, may I bring forgiveness.
Make Me an Instrument of Your Peace

REFLECTION. Forgiveness is the currency of Christianity. It is the core of the message. This is why patience and love are mentioned so often in the New Testament.

To bring forgiveness and reconciliation requires tremendous humility, patience, and faith.

PRAYER. *Bear with one another and forgive one another if anyone has reason to be offended with another. You must forgive just as the Lord has forgiven you.* (Col 3:13)

N THAT place where there is bitter dis-
agreement, may I bring about unity.

Make Me an Instrument of Your Peace

REFLECTION. The work of being an instrument
of God's peace is not for the faint of heart.

Paul is probably the best Christian unifier in
history, and yet, his ministry was full of challenges, which he met with unfailing strength
and endurance. Are you ready to be an instrument of God's peace?

PRAYER. *In everything we do, we present our-*
selves as ministers of God: in steadfast perse-
verance; afflictions, hardships, beatings, labors,
sleepless nights, and fasts, purity, knowledge,
patience and kindness. (2 Cor 6:4-6)

 N THAT place where there is error, may I
bring the truth.

Make Me an Instrument of Your Peace

REFLECTION. Speaking the truth is not the hard
part if you are steeped in Scripture and practic-
ing your faith. The real challenge is speaking
the truth in such a way that people will hear
and accept it.

To speak the truth in love is a gift of the Holy
Spirit at work in us.

PRAYER. *Only by speaking the truth in love can*
we mature in all ways to be like Christ, who is
our head. (Eph 4:15)

N THAT place where there is doubt, may I bring faith.

Make Me an Instrument of Your Peace

REFLECTION. Those who believe give everyone around them a shot in the arm.

The one who believes with a mature sense of confidence in God is a powerful witness to believers and unbelievers alike. Even Jesus Himself was impressed by those of great faith.

PRAYER. *When Jesus heard this he was amazed, and he said to those following him: "Amen, I tell you I have not found such great faith in anyone throughout Israel."* (Mt 8:10)

 N THAT place where there is despair, may I bring hope.

Make Me an Instrument of Your Peace

REFLECTION. To bring hope is a challenge for the average person because no one knows the future, and it is hard to assure someone that "everything will be all right." Will it?

Only by modeling firm faith in God, whatever the outcome, can we bring hope where there is despair.

PRAYER. *For I know well the plans I have in mind for you, says the Lord, plans for your welfare, not for woe. Plans to give you a future full of hope.* (Jer 29:11)

N THAT place where there are shadows, may I bring light.

Make Me an Instrument of Your Peace

REFLECTION. There is an old British phrase that described bad advice as, "wasting time and darkening counsel." Good advice has the opposite effect, shown in the phrase, "shedding light on the subject."

If our words are inspired by the Holy Spirit at work in us, we will be light in the darkness.

PRAYER. *He shines as a light for the upright in the darkness. Kindness, mercy, and justice are his hallmarks.* (Ps 112:4)

 N A place where there is sadness, may I bring joy.

Make Me an Instrument of Your Peace

REFLECTION. The most perfect and lasting joy you can bring into someone's life is to bring them Jesus, that is, to introduce to them the good news of the Gospel.

As we have seen in the writings of Francis, to bring Jesus to others was his only desire.

PRAYER. *You who bear good news, go up into the high mountains and say to the people: "Here is your God."* (Isa 40:9)

H MASTER, may I not seek so much to be consoled, as to console.

Make Me an Instrument of Your Peace

REFLECTION. The essence of Francis, and of all Christian Saints, is the way in which they have forgotten themselves in complete self-sacrifice to the service of others.

In our own day, we can think of Mother Teresa and Pope St. John Paul II as models for this complete pouring out of self.

PRAYER. *The Son of Man did not come to be served, but to serve, and to give his life as ransom for many.*

(Mt 20:28)

AY I seek not to be understood, so much as to understand.

Make Me an Instrument of Your Peace

REFLECTION. In the lifelong effort to be a humble servant, perhaps the last thing to go is the need to be justified. We want people to understand where we are coming from.

When we are ready to be misunderstood, mistreated, and slandered for the Gospel, we are approaching humility.

PRAYER. *He was despised and forsaken of men, a man of sorrows and acquainted with grief; And like one from whom men hide their face, he was despised, and we did not esteem him.*

(Isa 53:3)

MAY I seek not be loved so much as to love.

Make Me an Instrument of Your Peace

REFLECTION. It is good to remember that "love" is an active verb. To love, without worry about being loved in return, is heroic.

St. Stephen, the first martyr, exhibited this kind of love as he was being stoned to death.

PRAYER. *While they were stoning Stephen, he cried out in a clear voice, "Lord, do not hold this sin against them." And with those words he fell asleep.* (Acts 7:59-60)

T IS in giving that we receive, and losing ourselves that we find ourselves,

Make Me an Instrument of Your Peace

REFLECTION. Very early in life, a child learns to hold on—to parents, to possessions, to toys, and to what they want. That holding on is part of being a child.

Being grown up means learning to let it all go. Clinging to what we want prevents us from maturing as a person and as a Christian.

PRAYER. *Anyone who wishes to follow me must deny himself. Whoever wishes to save his life will lose it. But whoever loses his life for my sake will save it.* (Lk 9:23-24)

T IS in forgiving that we are forgiven, and it is in dying that we are brought to life eternal.

JULY
31

Make Me an Instrument of Your Peace

REFLECTION. If maturity requires letting go, then dying to ourselves is the complete letting go of everything.

Jesus assures us that the tremendously high cost of letting go of everything is worth the exchange.

PRAYER. *And if your eye causes you to sin, tear it out. It is preferable for you to enter into the Kingdom of God with one eye than to be cast into Gehenna with two eyes.* (Mk 9:47)

 F ANY brother, at the instigation of the enemy, sin mortally, let all the brothers not slander him, but let them have great mercy on him.

AUG.
1

To a Certain Minister

REFLECTION. Part of the motivation to know what is going on in the lives of others is natural human curiosity and a desire for some point of comparison.

But it so quickly becomes a matter of judging others, and assuring ourselves we are better than that.

PRAYER. *Do not judge, so that you in turn may not be judged.* (Mt 7:1)

AND if he should fall into any venial sin, let him confess to his brother priest, and if there be no priest there let him confess to his brother, until he shall find a priest who shall absolve him canonically.

AUG. 2

To a Certain Minister

REFLECTION. Talking to someone we trust about our faults and what is happening in our lives is a basic human need. This need explains the popularity of counseling.

Sacramental confession gives us so much more than someone to talk to. The power of the sacrament is a profound gift of God.

PRAYER. *Whatever you loose on earth will be loosed in heaven.* (Mt 18:18)

 CONSIDER and see that the day of death draws near.

AUG. 3

To the Rulers of the People

REFLECTION. When we bury the dead, the pain is very real. There is a finality in the death of a loved one that feels like something has changed forever.

In the midst of this pain, we sometimes contemplate the fact that we too will die and that the day of our death is rushing towards us, getting closer with every moment.

PRAYER. *For dust you are, and to dust you will return.* (Gen 3:19)

ASK you, therefore, with such reverence as I can, not to forget the Lord on account of the cares and solicitudes of this world and not to turn aside from His commandments.

AUG.
4

To the Rulers of the People

REFLECTION. The constant stream of information, messages, and images makes it hard to recall what we were doing just a moment ago.

"Do not forget the Lord" is Francis' advice to us. What presence of mind and sincere effort this requires!

PRAYER. *Someone hears the word, but the worries of life and the desire for wealth choke the word, and it produces nothing.*

(Mt 13:22)

 HEN the day of death comes, all which they think they have shall be taken away from them. And the more powerful they may have been in this world, so many greater torments shall they endure.

AUG.
5

To the Rulers of the People

REFLECTION. The world is full of reminders that fame, power, riches, and intelligence—all we strive for—is just temporary.

Walk through the ruins of Rome, or talk to an elderly loved one who cannot remember who you are, and know that everything we hold dear will be gone some day.

PRAYER. *The day is coming, burning like an oven, when all the arrogant and all evildoers will be stubble.*

(Mal 3:19)

117

I STRONGLY advise you, my lords, to put aside all care and solicitude and to receive readily the most holy Body and Blood of our Lord Jesus Christ. To the Rulers of the People

REFLECTION. The power of the Eucharist is one unchanging constant among all that is passing. From the time of Francis until today, the Eucharist continues to be an anchor.

The Eucharist can rightly be considered the center of our lives.

PRAYER. *The angel said: "Blessed are those who are invited to the wedding feast of the Lamb."* (Rev 19:9)

 C AUSE so great honor to be rendered the Lord by your people, that every evening it may be announced to the end that praises and thanks shall resound to the Lord God Almighty from all the people. To the Rulers of the People

REFLECTION. When people praise God, something unique is happening. They are turning their attention beyond all the things this world offers to focus on something greater than all of them.

When we praise God we experience His joy.

PRAYER. *Let the earth bless the Lord; praise and exalt him above all forever.* (Dan 3:74)

118

AND if you do not do this, know that you are beholden to render an account before your Lord God Jesus Christ on the Day of Judgment.

AUG.

8

To the Rulers of the People

REFLECTION. Accountability is a scary word. You may encounter it at work, or at the gym, or in a relationship. It means being responsible for our actions.

The ultimate accountability is due to the One Who made us, and Who is all powerful and omniscient.

PRAYER. *After a long period of time, the master of those servants returned and settled accounts with them.*

(Mt 25:19)

 I ENTREAT you that when it is becoming and expedient, you humbly beseech the clerics to venerate above all the most holy Body and Blood of our Lord Jesus Christ and His Holy Name.

AUG.

9

To All the Franciscan Superiors

REFLECTION. That Jesus is unique among all the characters of history is obvious, but that He has given us His Body and Blood and thereby remains with us is what makes Catholics unique.

In fact the longevity, the breadth, and the riches of the Catholic Church are so completely without equal that only Christ's presence in the Church can explain it.

PRAYER. *The living father sent me and I draw life from Him; so whoever feeds on me will also draw life from me.*

(Jn 6:57)

ND you shall so announce and preach **AUG.** His praise to all peoples that at every hour praise and thanks shall always **10** be given to the Almighty God by all the people through the whole earth.

To All the Franciscan Superiors

REFLECTION. There are many types of prayer, but the Bible refers to the prayer of praise more than any other. This is a point not to be missed.

Whereas other prayer types communicate with God, praise performs an act of worship to God.

PRAYER. *They cried out in a loud voice: "Salvation belongs to our God, who sits on the throne, and to the Lamb."* (Rev 7:10)

 N WHATEVER way it seems best to please **AUG.** the Lord God and to follow His footsteps **11** and poverty, so do with the blessing of the Lord God and in my obedience.

To Brother Leo

REFLECTION. Each of us is called to imitate the Lord Jesus Christ and follow in His footsteps guided by the Church and Scripture.

This is why there is such great diversity among the Saints, from Franciscans to Jesuits and so many in between.

PRAYER. *Jesus said to them, "Come, follow me."* (Mt 4:19)

UR Father, most holy, our Creator, Redeemer, and Comforter.

AUG.
12

The Praises

REFLECTION. In "The Praises," Francis expounds on the Our Father line by line.

In this reflection on the opening words, Francis calls to mind that every time we pray the Our Father we are addressing the whole trinity of persons in the Godhead: Father, Son, and Spirit.

PRAYER. *Heaven was opened and the Spirit of God descended like a dove upon him, and a voice from heaven said, "This is my Son, whom I love."* (Mt 3:16-17)

HO art in heaven, in the Angels and in the Saints illuminating them unto knowledge, for Thou, O Lord, art light; inflaming them unto love.

AUG.
13

The Praises

REFLECTION. Francis contemplates God in heaven with images of light and flame, which do not burn but which illuminate and inspire to Love, not unlike the sun.

And the brightness of heaven's glory is beyond the brightest day under the sun that we've ever known.

PRAYER. *The heavens declare the glory of God and the skies show forth his glory.* (Ps 19:1)

121

FOR Thou, O Lord, art Love; dwelling in them and filling them with blessedness, for Thou, O Lord, art the highest Good, the eternal Good from Whom is all good and without Whom is no good.

AUG.
14

The Praises

REFLECTION. At the center of heaven is God, and the Love of God filling everything.

Merely contemplating God's goodness and love, so perfect in heaven, brings down to our level some of that love—for we are what we think about most of the time.

PRAYER. *As we gaze upon the glory of the Lord we are being transformed into that same image from glory to glory.* (2 Cor 3:18)

---

*H*ALLOWED *be Thy Name*, may Thy knowledge shine in us that we may know the breadth of Thy benefits, the length of Thy promises, the height of Thy majesty, and the depth of Thy judgments.

AUG.
15

The Praises

REFLECTION. Making God's name holy is a perplexing thing for modern man to contemplate.

Francis suggests that making God's name holy is to know—and to experience—the grandeur of Who God is in all His greatness.

PRAYER. *The Mighty One has done great things for me, and holy is his name.* (Lk 1:49)

122

HY Kingdom come, that Thou may reign in us by grace and make us come to Thy Kingdom, where there is the clear vision, the perfect love, and the blessed company, and the eternal enjoyment of Thee. The Praises

REFLECTION. Think of all the leaders and significant people in your life. Politicians, parents, bosses, spouses, friends, etc.

Now imagine an all-loving, all-powerful, perfect God in those roles. That will be heaven.

PRAYER. *The government will rest on his shoulders and he will be called wonderful, counselor, mighty God, everlasting Father.* (Isa 9:5)

HY will be done on earth as it is in heaven, that we may love Thee with the whole heart by always thinking of Thee; with the whole soul by always desiring Thee; with the whole mind by directing all our intentions to Thee.

The Praises

REFLECTION. Francis interprets God's will with the idea of all His creatures following the great commandment: to love God with all our heart, soul, and mind.

To direct all of our self to God is to do God's will on earth.

PRAYER. *Love the Lord your God with all your heart, all your soul, all your mind, all your strength.* (Lk 10:27)

HY will be done on earth as it is in heaven, that we may love our neighbors even as ourselves, rejoicing in the good of others and giving offense to no one. **AUG. 18**
The Praises

REFLECTION. God's will being done on earth looks like everyone being good to each other.

But as humans, we know that getting along with one another can only be accomplished with the help of the Holy Spirit.

PRAYER. *There shall be no harm or ruin on my holy mountain, for the earth shall be filled with the knowledge of the Lord as the waters cover the sea.* (Isa 11:9)

 IVE us this day, through memory and understanding and reverence for the love which He had for us—our daily bread, Thy Beloved Son, our Lord Jesus Christ. **AUG. 19**
The Praises

REFLECTION. There are many ways to interpret "our daily bread." It can represent the food and finances we need for a day, or the spiritual sustenance of His word, or the Eucharist of daily Mass.

Receiving our daily bread starts with remembering, understanding, and reverencing Christ.

PRAYER. *You open wide your hand and grant the desires of all who live.* (Ps 145:16)

124

ND forgive us our trespasses, by Thy mercy in virtue of the Passion of Thy Beloved Son, our Lord Jesus Christ, and through the intercession of the most Blessed Virgin Mary and of all Thy Saints. **AUG. 20** *The Praises*

REFLECTION. The beauty of the Christian world view is that we all work together to help each other to attain our greatest good.

The concept of intercession starts with Jesus' death for us, but it continues in all the works and prayers of all the Christians who ever lived.

PRAYER. *Christ Jesus, who died and who was raised to life is at the right hand of the Father, interceding for us.* (Rom 8:34)

 S WE forgive those that trespass against us, and what we do not fully forgive, do Thou, O Lord, make us fully forgive, that for Thy sake we may truly love our enemies and intercede for them. **AUG. 21** *The Praises*

REFLECTION. The Lord's Prayer is made up mostly of petitions, but it sneaks in a promise that we will forgive those who have hurt us. Francis adds the idea that we will also pray for them.

It was Christ Himself Who urged us not only to forgive those who have hurt us, but to pray for their good.

PRAYER. *But I say to you, love your enemies, and pray for those who persecute you.* (Mt 5:44)

125

S WE *forgive those that trespass against us,* **that we may render no evil for evil, but in Thee may strive to do good to all.** The Praises

AUG. 22

REFLECTION. There is only one clause in the Our Father that has a condition—the forgiveness clause.

If we want to be forgiven, we must always forgive. God will not accept hypocrisy.

PRAYER. *You hypocrite! First remove the wooden plank from your own eye, then you will see clearly to take the speck out of your neighbor's eye.* (Mt 7:5)

ND *lead us not into temptation,* **hidden or visible, sudden or continuous.** The Praises

AUG. 23

REFLECTION. Temptation comes in so many forms, and is such a constant in our lives, that it is easy to miss the vast majority of temptations and only to focus on the major moments of testing.

To be perfect is to face and overcome temptation minute by minute.

PRAYER. *The end of all things is near. Therefore, lead disciplined lives and be watchful in prayer.* (1 Pet 4:7)

UT *deliver us from evil,* past, present, and to come. Amen. **AUG. 24** The Praises

REFLECTION. Just as God's love permeates the universe and is always reaching out to find us, so the malice of our enemy is always searching for us.

We must strive to overcome evil, but even our best efforts will require God's help.

PRAYER. *The Lord said to Satan, "Where did you come from?" Satan answered, "From prowling about on the earth, going back and forth on it."*

(Job 1:7)

 LMIGHTY, most holy, most high, and supreme God, highest good, all good, wholly good, Who alone art good. To Thee we render all praise, all glory, all thanks, all honor, all blessing, and we shall always refer all good to Thee. Amen. **AUG. 25** The Praises

REFLECTION. We can see Francis straining to express the fullness of all God is, and all God deserves from us.

If we slowly take in each word of this praise, we will see God through the eyes of a man who knew God as well as a human can know Him.

PRAYER. *Praise and glory, wisdom and thanksgiving, honor and power and might, be to our God forever and ever. Amen.*

(Rev 7:12)

127

T IS to be strictly observed that any friar who uttered idle words, shall say one Our Father, praising God at the beginning and end of the prayer; and if conscious of his fault he accuse himself. **AUG. 26**

The Praises

REFLECTION. For Francis, repeating the Our Father, with praises before and after, was a way to make atonement for our sins.

Like washing a dish, devout reciting of the Our Father can cleanse us to begin again.

PRAYER. *Let the words of my mouth and the thoughts of my heart find favor in your sight, O Lord, my Rock and my Redeemer.* *(Ps 19:15)*

 AIL, holy Lady, most holy Queen, Mother of God, Mary who art ever Virgin, chosen from Heaven by the most Holy Father, **AUG. 27**

Salutation of the Blessed Virgin

REFLECTION. All of the Saints and many Popes had a deep devotion to the Virgin Mary.

The famous Benedictine Monk Thomas Merton's only regret was that he did not develop a devotion to Mary sooner in his life.

PRAYER. *The angel came to her and said, "Hail, full of grace! The Lord is with you."* *(Lk 1:28)*

AIL, holy Lady, whom He has conse-
crated with the most holy beloved
Son and the Ghostly Paraclete, in
whom was and is all the fullness of
grace and all good.

Salutation of the Blessed Virgin

REFLECTION. Angels generally do not venerate those they visit in Scripture, rather, they are shown respect and veneration.

It is different with Mary. Gabriel humbles himself before her. This is a very unique moment in Scripture!

PRAYER. *Then the angel said to her, "Do not be afraid, Mary, for you have found favor with God."* (Lk 1:30)

AIL thou His palace! Hail thou His
tabernacle! Hail thou His house. Hail
thou His garment! Hail thou His hand-
maiden! Salutation of the Blessed Virgin

REFLECTION. Like the Ark of the Covenant, or the Tabernacle, or a Church or the Temple, Mary is the house where God's glory dwells.

Just the physical ramifications of carrying God in one's body give a glimpse of Mary's unique position.

PRAYER. *"Behold, you will conceive in your womb and bear a son, and you will name him Jesus."* (Lk 1:31)

HAIL thou His Mother and all your holy virtues which by the grace and illumination of the Holy Ghost you impart into the hearts of the faithful.

AUG. 30

Salutation of the Blessed Virgin

REFLECTION. All the Saints are models for us to imitate, and even more, benefactors, who share with us their merits and holiness.

Mary, more than all other Saints, embodies the Christian merits and virtues we strive for.

PRAYER. *The Holy Spirit will come upon you, and the power of the most high will overshadow you.* (Lk 1:35)

BLESSED is the servant who always continues under the rod of correction.

AUG. 31

Admonitions, 24

REFLECTION. The key word here is "continues." To take correction and not make an excuse, not retaliate in kind, not quit, walk away, or give up requires the patience of a Saint.

It is a powerful demonstration of faithfulness, and it is the ultimate test of our self-control as well. Unlike many habits that are formed by word and deed, true humility is formed in silence and self-denial.

PRAYER. *Like a lamb that is silent before its shearer, he did not open his mouth. In his humiliation, justice was denied him.* (Acts 8:32-33)

LESSED is the brother who would love and fear his brother as much when he is far from him as he would when with him, and who would not say anything about him behind his back that he could not with charity say in his presence. **SEPT. 1**

Admonitions, 25

REFLECTION. As we make our way through Francis' admonitions, we get the impression that sanctity requires a great deal of focus.

Most Christian behavior is counter to our self-centered instincts and our natural reactions.

PRAYER. *Remain sober and alert, for your enemy, the devil, is on the prowl like a roaring lion, looking for someone to devour.* *(1 Pet 5:8)*

 HERE there is charity and wisdom there is neither fear nor ignorance. **SEPT. 2**

Admonitions, 27

REFLECTION. Those who live in love have a wisdom about them, particularly in their sense of priorities. They know what is important.

Those who are fearful see things that aren't there, and tend not to grasp the truth when it is presented to them.

PRAYER. *In love there is no fear; indeed, perfect love casts out fear.* *(1 Jn 4:18)*

HERE there is mercy and discretion there is neither superfluity nor hard-heartedness. **SEPT. 3**

Admonitions, 27

REFLECTION. Mercy can be thought of as widening our judgment enough to include the possibility that, even in their brokenness, others still deserve our love.

Discretion, on the other hand, is a careful measuring of our actions that guides our acts of charity to their highest and best use.

PRAYER. *O Lord, you are kind and forgiving, filled with kindness for all who cry to you.*

(Ps 86:5)

 HERE there is patience and humility there is neither anger nor worry. **SEPT. 4**

Admonitions, 27

REFLECTION. Humility and patience could be synonyms. They both require us to overcome our self-centeredness.

If we can do that—stop focusing on what we want—it's no surprise that we would no longer feel angry or worried about circumstances getting in the way.

PRAYER. *Wait quietly for the Lord and be patient until he comes. Refrain from anger, and turn away from wrath. Do not fret—it does nothing but harm.* *(Ps 37:7-8)*

HERE there is poverty and joy there is neither cupidity nor avarice. **SEPT. 5**
Admonitions, 27

REFLECTION. Human beings are tremendously adaptable. They can make do with very little. It is not uncommon to find out that when we do have less, we are often happier.

The idea that we will only be happy if we have more, always more, doesn't seem to stand up to the reality of our experience.

PRAYER. *Better is a little with fear of the Lord, than great treasures without content.*

(Prov 15:16)

HERE there is quiet and meditation there is neither worry nor waste. **SEPT. 6**
Admonitions, 27

REFLECTION. How many of our troubles do we bring upon ourselves because we are unable to stay quietly in our own space?

St. Augustine spoke of this restlessness without God when he said, "Our hearts are restless until they rest in thee."

PRAYER. *Blessed is the man who does not walk in the counsel of the wicked, nor stand in the way of sinners, nor sit in the company of scoffers. Rather, his delight is in the law of the Lord and he meditates on that law day and night.*

(Ps 1:1-2)

HERE there is the fear of the Lord to guard the house the enemy cannot find a way to enter.

Admonitions, 27

REFLECTION. There is a lot of confusion over the phrase "fear of the Lord."

If it means no more than "obedience" and having enough respect for God that you will not do anything to offend Him, that would be a good start.

PRAYER. *Fear of the Lord is the beginning of wisdom, and the knowledge of the Holy One leads to understanding.* (Prov 9:10)

 LESSED is the servant who keeps the secrets of the Lord in his heart.

Admonitions, 28

REFLECTION. Whatever we hold in our hearts, we hold dear. We rarely forget something when we have committed to hold it in our heart.

All that God teaches us and shares with us should be learned "by heart" so that we can draw upon it when we need it.

PRAYER. *I have hidden your words in my heart, so that I might remember not to sin against you.* (Ps 119:11)

AIL, Queen Wisdom! May the Lord save thee with thy sister holy pure simplicity. O Lady, holy poverty, may the Lord save thee with thy sister, holy humility! O Lady, holy charity, may the Lord save thee with thy sister holy obedience! Salutation of the Virtues

REFLECTION. Wisdom, simplicity, poverty, humility, obedience: for Francis, they are all related, so that when one welcomes them into one's life, these shining virtues dwell together as family.

PRAYER. *Supplement your faith with virtue, and virtue with knowledge, and knowledge with self-control, and self-control with endurance, and endurance with piety.* (2 Pet 1:5-6)

E WHO possesses one [of the virtues] and does not offend the others, possesses all; and he who offends one, possesses none and offends all; and every one of them confounds vices and sins. Salutation of the Virtues

REFLECTION. As with so many things, the virtues are organic—they rely on each other. They grow up together and have an interdependent relationship.

Obedience requires patience and patience requires humility, and so on.

PRAYER. *If anyone thinks that he is religious but does not restrain his tongue, he is deceiving himself and his religion is worthless.* (Jas 1:26)

OLY wisdom confounds Satan and all his wickedness. Pure holy simplicity confounds all the wisdom of this world and the wisdom of the flesh.

Salutation of the Virtues

REFLECTION. Being extremely intelligent, or even very street smart, can feed our ego and often make us critical or condescending.

God's wisdom is so different from the kinds of learning we achieve as humans.

PRAYER. *The wisdom that comes from above is first of all pure, then peaceable, gentle, and considerate, full of mercy and good fruits, without any trace of partiality or hypocrisy.* (Jas 3:17)

 OLY humility confounds pride and all the men of this world and all things that are in the world.

Salutation of the Virtues

REFLECTION. The desire to possess, consume, and control are a sort of default nature that get in the way of holiness.

We can fight these vices head on, but through humility we can walk away from them, and leave them behind.

PRAYER. *Daily life in this world—the things our flesh lusts after, the things our eyes covet, and the pride of being alive—these do not come from the Father, but are a result of living in the world.* (1 Jn 2:16)

OLY charity confounds all diabolical **SEPT.** and fleshly temptations and all fleshly fears. Salutation of the Virtues **13**

REFLECTION. Love is the answer to everything. And everyone agrees, from the most exalted literature to the simplest Country and Western song.

Charitable, self-sacrificing love is the highest and most productive activity a human can achieve.

PRAYER. *Love is patient; love is charitable. Love is not envious; it does not have an inflated opinion of itself; it is not filled with its own importance.* (1 Cor 13:4)

 OLY obedience confounds all bodily **SEPT.** and fleshly desires and keeps the body mortified to the obedience of the spirit **14** and to the obedience to all the men of this world. Salutation of the Virtues

REFLECTION. Obedience that is virtuous goes far beyond simply following commands, it is putting another's wishes before ours.

This is perhaps the most difficult thing we can do. And that is exactly why it is so effective for growing in holiness.

PRAYER. *Your obedience has become known to all and has caused me to rejoice greatly over you.* (Rom 16:19)

T SEEMED to me very bitter to see lepers, **SEPT.** and the Lord Himself led me amongst them and I showed them mercy. And when **15** I left them, that which had seemed to me bitter was changed into sweetness.

Testament of Holy Father Francis

REFLECTION. We get used to having a "virtual" knowledge of so many things in life.

It is important for every Christian to see, meet, and make physical contact with the poor at some point.

PRAYER. *Whoever oppresses the poor insults his maker, but he who is kind to the needy honors him.*

(Prov 14:31)

 HE Lord gave me so much faith in **SEPT.** churches that I would simply pray and say thus: "We adore Thee Lord Jesus **16** Christ here and in all Thy churches which are in the whole world."

Testament of Holy Father Francis

REFLECTION. The Catholic Church is the organization to which Christ entrusted His ongoing physical presence in the world.

This is most true in the presence of Christ in the Eucharist in all the tabernacles in all the Catholic Churches in the world.

PRAYER. *And behold, I am with you always, to the end of the world.*

(Mt 28:20)

THE Lord gave me so much faith in priests who live according to the form of the holy Roman Church, on account of their order, that if they should persecute me, I would still turn to them.

SEPT. 17

Testament of Holy Father Francis

REFLECTION. Francis had a deep devotion to the Sacraments, especially the Holy Eucharist.

This devotion, along with Francis' complete sense of obedience to the Catholic Church, helped to fuel his deep respect for the priesthood.

PRAYER. *Obey your leaders and submit to them, for they watch over your souls and will have to render an account in that regard.* (Heb 13:17)

 IF I had as much wisdom as Solomon had, and if I should find poor priests of this world, I would not preach against their will in the parishes in which they live.

SEPT. 18

Testament of Holy Father Francis

REFLECTION. As with all the Saints, Francis lived out his humility by his submission to authority and to the laws of the Catholic Church.

An appropriate respect for the priesthood is foundational to our submission to the Catholic faith.

PRAYER. *Presbyters who do their duty well should be considered deserving of a double honor, especially those who labor at preaching and teaching.* (1 Tim 5:17)

139

AND I desire to fear, love, and honor [priests] and all others as my masters; and I do not wish to consider sin in them, for in them I see the Son of God and they are my masters. SEPT. **19**

Testament of Holy Father Francis

REFLECTION. The painful truth is that perhaps no one's faults are more publicly celebrated today than the Catholic priest's.

We ought to pray for them daily. They are God's chosen instruments to bring us Jesus in the Sacraments. They do so at great personal cost.

PRAYER. *"Do you dare to insult God's high priest?" Paul replied, "Brethren, I did not realize that he was the high priest. It is clearly written, 'You shall not curse the ruler of your people.'"* (Acts 23:4-5)

———————

 IN THIS world, I see nothing corporally of the Most High Son of God Himself except His most holy Body and Blood. And I will that these most holy mysteries be honored and revered above all things. SEPT. **20**

Testament of Holy Father Francis

REFLECTION. Francis understood, as the Catechism teaches, that the Eucharist is the source and summit of our faith.

PRAYER. *Then the angel said to me, "Write: 'Blessed are those who are invited to the wedding banquet of the Lamb.'" And he added, "These are the true words of God."* (Rev 19:9)

E OUGHT to honor and venerate all theologians and those who minister to us the most holy Divine Words as those who minister to us spirit and life.

Testament of Holy Father Francis

REFLECTION. Everyone we meet deserves our love and respect, but those who bring us the Word of God should inspire us with joy and engender a special appreciation.

PRAYER. *How beautiful upon the mountains are the feet of those who bring good news, and who speak of peace: of those that show forth good, that preach salvation, that say to believers: Your God reigns!* (Isa 52:7)

 HEREVER I find His most holy Names and written words in unseemly places, I wish to collect them, and I ask that they may be collected and put in a becoming place.

Testament of Holy Father Francis

REFLECTION. A Saint's devotion to God is complete in that it drives him to desire that honor, devotion, and respect for God to extend beyond the Church to the entire world.

PRAYER. *May my mouth declare the praise of the Lord, and may every creature bless his holy name forever and ever.* (Ps 145:21)

ND when the Lord gave me some **SEPT.** brothers, no one showed me what I ought to do, but the Most High Himself revealed to me that I should live according to the form of the holy **Gospel.** Testament of Holy Father Francis

SEPT. 23

REFLECTION. We treasure the faith that is passed down to us by our parents and grandparents, but as mature Christians we also must learn to discern the Holy Spirit teaching and guiding us directly.

This requires prayer, fasting, and obedience.

PRAYER. *Those who are led by the Spirit of God are children of God.* (Rom 8:14)

 WORKED with my hands and I wish to **SEPT.** work, and I wish firmly that all the other brothers should work at some labor which is compatible with honesty.

SEPT. 24

Testament of Holy Father Francis

REFLECTION. The life of the monk is summed up in two words *Ora et labora*—that is, pray and work. These are two activities that keep us safe from temptation.

When we are praying or working we are least likely to sin.

PRAYER. *With toil and drudgery we worked day and night so that we would not burden any of you.* (2 Thes 3:8)

ET those who know not [how to work] **SEPT.** learn, not through desire to receive the price of labor but for the sake of example and to repel idleness. **25**

Testament of Holy Father Francis

REFLECTION. The Bible has much to say about the importance of working hard.

Though we may rarely hear hard work spoken of along with the other virtues, it is clearly an important Christian trait.

PRAYER. *I have shown you that by such hard work we must help the weak.* (Acts 20:35)

 HE Lord revealed to me this salutation, that we should say: "The Lord give thee peace." **SEPT.** **26**

Testament of Holy Father Francis

REFLECTION. The "passing of the peace" is an ancient Christian custom, and it goes back even into the Hebrew tradition where the common word of greeting, *Shalom*, means "peace be with you."

The desire to give peace to those whom we come in contact with should be carefully considered before we even open our mouth to say hello.

PRAYER. *Blessed are the peacemakers, they will be called children of God.* (Mt 5:9)

143

I STRICTLY enjoin by obedience on all the **SEPT.** brothers that they should not dare to ask **27** for any letter from the Roman curia either for a church or for any other place, nor under pretext of preaching, nor on account of persecution.

Testament of Holy Father Francis

REFLECTION. When you think of how powerful the desire is to own our own home, and the house pride you see in your neighbors, you begin to grasp the tremendous sacrifice required to live the Franciscan virtue of poverty.

PRAYER. *The Son of Man has nowhere to lay his head.* *(Lk 9:58)*

 T HE Lord has given me to speak and to **SEPT.** write the Rule and these words simply **28** and purely, so shall you understand them simply and purely and observe them until the end.

Testament of Holy Father Francis

REFLECTION. The Saints all shared the purity and simplicity that Francis speaks of, but that does not mean they were idle.

Holy simplicity is not a lack of things to do, but an inner calm that influences how everything is done.

PRAYER. *Even though our outer self is continuing to decay, our inner self is being renewed day by day.* *(2 Cor 4:16)*

HOEVER shall observe these things may he be filled in heaven with the blessing of the Most High Father and may he be filled on earth with the blessing of His Beloved Son together with the Holy Ghost.

Testament of Holy Father Francis

REFLECTION. When you do the works of holiness, you receive the blessings of heaven.

But then, it is a blessing of heaven to be able to do the works of holiness in the first place.

PRAYER. *Work out your salvation with fear and trembling, for it is God who is working in you.*

(Phil 2:12-13)

 ND I, Brother Francis, your little one and servant, in so far as I am able, I confirm to you within and without, this most holy blessing. Amen.

Testament of Holy Father Francis

REFLECTION. Francis called himself, "the little one" and his order, "the Friars minor."

With Saints, it seems the more they grow in holiness, the less they seek greatness. As they rise, they fall. As they become truly great, they get smaller.

PRAYER. *Do not act out of selfish ambition or vanity, but humbly regard others as better than yourselves. Be concerned not only with your own interests but also with those of others.*

(Phil 2:3-4)

T O ALL Christians, religious, cleric, laics, men and women, who dwell in the whole world, Brother Francis presents reverent homage, wishing true peace from heaven and sincere charity in the Lord.
Letter to All the Faithful

OCT.
1

REFLECTION. In his old age, unable to travel, Francis took to letter writing, which, like his preaching, was aimed at everyone who would hear.

Like him, we must use every means possible to tell about Jesus.

PRAYER. *Then he said to them, "Go forth into the whole world, and proclaim the gospel to all creation."* (Mk 16:15)

B EING the servant of all, I am bound to serve all and to administer the balm-bearing words of my Lord.
Letter to All the Faithful

OCT.
2

REFLECTION. As with all the Saints, Francis exhibits a zeal and passion for talking about Jesus that makes him "bound" to serve others as their servant.

Our faith should exert this kind of hold over us and drive us to good works.

PRAYER. *Although I am free and belong to no man, I have made myself a slave to all so as to win over as many as possible.* (1 Cor 9:19)

146

CONSIDERING the weakness of my body, I propose by letter to offer you the words of our Lord Jesus Christ, the Word of the Father and the words of the Holy Ghost which are "spirit and life." **OCT. 3**
Letter to All the Faithful

REFLECTION. One of God's many gifts to us is the varied ways that we can experience Him—as a Father, as a man in Jesus, and in a continuing presence we know as the Holy Spirit.

How will God reveal Himself to you today?

PRAYER. *Go, therefore, . . . baptizing in the name of the Father and of the Son and of the Holy Spirit.*
(Mt 28:19)

THIS Word of the Father the most High announced from heaven by His holy archangel Gabriel to the holy and glorious Virgin Mary in whose womb He received the true flesh of our humanity. **OCT. 4**
Letter to All the Faithful

REFLECTION. In his letter, Francis reviews the key points of our faith, starting with the Virgin birth.

Francis does this because we can never take for granted and never stop professing these foundational principles of Christianity.

PRAYER. *Keep alert; stand firm in the faith; be courageous; be strong.*
(1 Cor 16:13)

H E, BEING rich above all, willed, nevertheless, with His most Blessed Mother, to choose poverty.

Letter to All the Faithful

REFLECTION. Voluntary poverty, like voluntary fasting, is one of the ways that many Saints have used to draw closer to God.

Through it, we more closely imitate Jesus, Whose very life was a model for us to study and apply, however we can, to our own lives.

PRAYER. *For you are well aware of the grace of our Lord Jesus Christ. Although he was rich, he became poor for your sake, so that by his poverty, you might become rich.* (2 Cor 8:9)

T AKING bread, He gave thanks and blessed and broke it saying: "Take and eat: this is My Body." And, taking the chalice, He said: "This is My Blood of the New Testament, which shall be shed for you and for many unto remission of sins."

Letter to All the Faithful

REFLECTION. Among the many passages in the Bible which are at the heart of our faith, we find these words.

Francis shares them in his letter to underscore the tremendous importance of the Lord's Supper, the Eucharist.

PRAYER. *And so, whenever you eat this bread and drink this cup, you proclaim the death of the Lord until he comes.* (1 Cor 11:26)

AFTER that He prayed to the Father, saying: "Father, if it be possible, let this chalice pass from Me." And His sweat became as drops of blood, trickling down upon the ground.

OCT.
7

Letter to All the Faithful

REFLECTION. As you go through your day, the humdrum, the dramatic, and the intense, remind yourself, "Jesus sweat blood for this."

Whatever you may think of your day, every moment was of great value to Him, and worth suffering for.

PRAYER. *For God did not send his son into the world to condemn the world, but in order that the world might be saved through him.* (Jn 3:17)

NEVERTHELESS, He gave up His will to the will of the Father, saying: "Father, Thy will be done: not as I will, but as Thou will."

OCT.
8

Letter to All the Faithful

REFLECTION. Jesus is always to be a model for us, but perhaps nowhere is His example clearer than in these words: "not my will, but thine."

Because of our ego, this is probably the most difficult example for us to follow.

PRAYER. *Although he was a Son, he learned obedience through his sufferings.* (Heb 5:8)

149

UCH was the will of the Father that His **OCT. 9** Son whom He gave to us, and who was born for us, should by His own Blood, sacrifice, and oblation, offer Himself on the altar of the Cross.

Letter to All the Faithful

REFLECTION. If we were planning the Incarnation, we would probably have kept death out of it altogether, or at least have the Son die a peaceful death.

Jesus' obedience to death on a Cross has won for us eternal life. Who can ask for anything more?

PRAYER. *He did not spare his own Son but gave him up for all of us. How then can he fail to give us everything else along with him?* (Rom 8:32)

HOW happy and blessed are those **OCT. 10** who love the Lord, who do as the Lord says in the Gospel: "Thou shall love the Lord thy God with thy whole heart and with thy whole soul." Letter to All the Faithful

REFLECTION. Young love is such a joyful thing.

It is no different when we are blessed to achieve a burning love for our Lord and God. Everything is more beautiful, more meaningful, and more joyful, for indeed we are in love with Love itself.

PRAYER. *My beloved is mine, and I am his.*

(Song 2:16)

ET us therefore love God and adore Him with a pure heart and a pure mind because He Himself, seeking that above all, says: "The true adorers shall adore the Father in spirit and in truth." **OCT. 11**

Letter to All the Faithful

REFLECTION. To worship in spirit and truth can seem a high and lofty goal that we could not obtain.

Perhaps we can start by pondering its opposite. What would it mean to be praying or at Mass "in the flesh and in falsehood"?

PRAYER. *Leave your gift there at the altar and first go to be reconciled with your brother, then return and offer your gift.* (Mt 5:24)

ND let us offer Him praises and prayers day and night, saying: "Our Father who art in heaven," for "we ought always to pray, and not to faint." **OCT. 12**

Letter to All the Faithful

REFLECTION. Catholics have been pondering for 2000 years how to "pray always."

One answer is constant, interior prayer, through the repetition to ourselves of the Jesus Prayer, "Jesus, Son of God, have mercy on me, a sinner."

PRAYER. *You are to be renewed in the spirit of your minds.* (Eph 4:23)

151

E OUGHT indeed to confess all our sins to a priest and receive from him the Body and Blood of our Lord Jesus Christ. He who does not eat His Flesh and does not drink His Blood cannot enter into the Kingdom of God.

OCT. 13

Letter to All the Faithful

REFLECTION. What a blessing to have access to the Eucharist! Through daily Mass the Church makes it possible for us to receive "our daily bread."

But let's not forget about confession. Francis considers them as going together.

PRAYER. *Give us each day our daily bread.*

(Lk 11:3)

———————

 ET us, moreover, "bring forth fruits worthy of penance." And let us love our neighbors as ourselves, and, if any one does not wish to love them, let him at least do them no harm.

OCT. 14

Letter to All the Faithful

REFLECTION. Living up to the standard of real, self-sacrificing love is not always possible.

At least we can start by refraining from those things that offend against love, like anger, impatience, unkindness, cruel words, and gossip.

PRAYER. *Remove all forms of bitterness and wrath and anger and shouting and slander, as well as all malice from your lives.* *(Eph 4:31)*

FOR let judgment without mercy be shown to him that does not show mercy.

Letter to All the Faithful

OCT.
15

REFLECTION. It's easy to miss the fact, but Jesus says over and over again that we control the harshness of our own judgment by how we judge others.

Indeed, this concept leads to the only statement in the Our Father that has a condition: "forgive us our debts as we forgive our debtors."

PRAYER. *For you will be treated as you treat others. The standard you use in judging is the standard by which you will be judged.* (Mt 7:2)

LET us then have charity and humility and let us give alms because they wash souls from the foulness of sins.

Letter to All the Faithful

OCT.
16

REFLECTION. Another way in which God allows us to control the harshness of our judgment is in the constant promises that our actions on earth will be considered on the last day.

We must not miss any opportunity to do good or to show love toward another.

PRAYER. *Above all, maintain the fervor of your love for one another, because love covers a multitude of sins.* (1 Pet 4:8)

FOR men lose all which they leave in this world; they carry with them, however, the reward of charity and alms which they have given, for which they shall receive a recompense from the Lord.

Letter to All the Faithful

REFLECTION. We know the saying, "you can't take it with you." but there are some things which You cannot leave behind.

The way in which you treat others on earth will be carefully considered after our death.

PRAYER. *Mercy and truth will atone for sin, and by the fear of the Lord men avoid evil.* (Prov 16:6)

WE OUGHT also to fast and to abstain from vices and sins and from superfluity of food and drink, and to be Catholics.

Letter to All the Faithful

REFLECTION. We live in a time of excess. Despite the poverty that remains in our world, for most of us, hunger doesn't stand a chance in our lives.

Self-imposed limits on our desires will benefit not just our bodies, but our souls as well.

PRAYER. *I discipline my body and bring it under control, for fear that after preaching to others I myself may be disqualified.* (1 Cor 9:27)

WE OUGHT also to visit churches frequently and to reverence clerics on account of their office and administration of the most holy Body and Blood of our Lord Jesus Christ. Letter to All the Faithful

REFLECTION. Though churches are not usually left unlocked anymore, there's nothing to stop us from ringing the rectory doorbell and asking to be let in to pray.

There was a time when Catholic children were taught that Jesus liked to have visitors to His home.

PRAYER. *I will bring them to my holy mountain, and make them joyful in my house of prayer.* *(Isa 56:7)*

AND let us all know for certain that no one can be saved except by the Blood of our Lord Jesus Christ and by the holy words of the Lord which clerics say and which they alone administer and not others.

Letter to All the Faithful

REFLECTION. When one goes back to the original writings of Francis, it is hard to miss his focus on the Eucharist and the priesthood.

This fits well with his reverence for creation and the physical world, for the Eucharist is the physical presence of Christ among us.

PRAYER. *For my flesh is real food, and my blood is real drink.* *(Jn 6:55)*

E OUGHT to hate our bodies with [their] vices and sins, because the Lord says in the Gospel that all vices and sins come forth from the heart.

OCT. 21

Letter to All the Faithful

REFLECTION. We know that Catholics emphasize the goodness of God's creation over the fall, but no one can deny the battle that goes on between flesh and spirit.

This is why fasting and self-denial have always been part of Catholic spirituality.

PRAYER. *For the desires of the flesh are opposed to the Spirit, and those of the Spirt are opposed to the flesh.* *(Gal 5:17)*

 E OUGHT to love our enemies and do good to them that hate us. We ought to observe the precepts and counsels of our Lord Jesus Christ.

OCT. 22

Letter to All the Faithful

REFLECTION. There's a reason these two sentences go together. In observing the precepts and counsels of Jesus, this love of enemies may be the most difficult.

When we love our enemies, we demonstrate how we love our Lord.

PRAYER. *But I say to you, love your enemies. Pray for those who persecute you.* *(Mt 5:44)*

156

AND let him not be angry with a brother on account of his offense, but advise him kindly and encourage him with all patience and humility.

OCT. 23

Letter to All the Faithful

REFLECTION. When it comes to getting along with our friends and family, treating them with patience and humility is the key.

To be patient and humble when others offend us is a sign of spiritual maturity.

PRAYER. *Anxiety in the heart makes one depressed, but a good word will bring good cheer.*

(Prov 12:25)

 WE OUGHT not to be "wise according to the flesh" and prudent, but we ought rather to be simple, humble, and pure.

OCT. 24

Letter to All the Faithful

REFLECTION. Once again we see the duality between the spirit and the flesh. As Christians we need to be sensitive to the two natures at work in us.

The Franciscan way of discerning between spirit and flesh is to starve the flesh, to challenge and subdue it through fasting and self-denial. In this way we reduce our dependence upon the material world and begin to recognize the Spirit at work within us.

PRAYER. *I advise you to be guided by the Spirit so that you will not gratify the desires of the flesh.*

(Gal 5:16)

WE SHOULD never desire to be above others, but ought rather to be servants and subject to every human creature for God's sake. OCT. 25

Letter to All the Faithful

REFLECTION. This is the genius of the Franciscan charism, it has figured out how to lead by serving, and how to be the greatest by being the least.

It has captured the paradoxes of Christianity: When you lose yourself, you find yourself. When you are poor, you are rich.

PRAYER. *For the foolishness of God is wiser than human wisdom.* (1 Cor 1:25)

THE Spirit of the Lord shall rest upon all those who do these things and who shall persevere to the end, and He shall make His abode and dwelling in them, and they shall be children of the heavenly Father. OCT. 26

Letter to All the Faithful

REFLECTION. If it could be promised that those who obey Jesus would receive a million dollars in the mail, a great many of us would give it a good try.

But to have the Spirit come live in us, and to have fellowship with the Trinity is so much greater than money!

PRAYER. *To me, your love is better than life itself. I will praise you.* (Ps 63:4)

WE ARE spouses [of our Lord] when by the Holy Ghost the faithful soul is united to Jesus Christ.

OCT. **27**

Letter to All the Faithful

REFLECTION. To receive the Holy Spirit is to share in the divine life of the Trinity.

The Trinity is a relationship of love between the three divine persons, and when we receive the Holy Spirit we share in that love.

PRAYER. *The love of God has been poured into our hearts through the Holy Spirit that has been given to us.* (Rom 5:5b)

WE ARE His brothers when we do the will of His Father Who is in heaven.

OCT. **28**

Letter to All the Faithful

REFLECTION. Being part of a family includes the sharing of values, character, and goals. To be a child of God is to voluntarily behave according to the family's values.

It all begins, however, with firmly believing in Jesus and desiring to follow His example.

PRAYER. *Whoever does the will of my heavenly Father is my brother and sister and mother.*

(Mt 12:50)

E ARE His mother when we bear Him in our heart and in our body through pure love and a clean conscience and we bring Him forth by holy work which ought to shine as an example to others.

Letter to All the Faithful

REFLECTION. Being chosen to carry Jesus in her womb clearly makes Mary the most blessed of all human creatures. And yet, we, too, can bring Jesus to the world.

Carrying Jesus to the world begins with making a fitting home for Him in our hearts.

PRAYER. *Revere Christ as Lord in your hearts. Always be prepared to offer an explanation to anyone who asks you to justify the hope that is in you.* *(1 Pet 3:15)*

 HOW glorious and holy and great to have a Father in heaven! O how holy, fair, and lovable to have a spouse in heaven!

Letter to All the Faithful

REFLECTION. This theme of family and relationships runs throughout the entire Bible. From Adam and Eve, to Father Abraham, all the way to the Holy Family and the Supper of the Lamb in Revelation.

Our faith relies in so many ways upon our ability to enter into relationship.

PRAYER. *I will walk among you. I will be your God, and you will be my people.* *(Lev 26:12)*

FTEN Francis would say: "When a servant of God is praying and is visited by a new consolation he should say to the Lord: 'This sweetness you have sent from heaven, Lord, to me, an unworthy sinner, and I return it to you so that you may keep it for me.'" Celano, Second Life, Chapter 65

REFLECTION. The offering of all things to God is a popular Catholic practice which many do in the morning offering.

Francis realized that when God exalted him, or gave him more suffering, these were not done for Francis' sake, but to glorify God.

PRAYER. *Everything comes from you, and we have given you only what comes from your hand.* (1 Chr 29:14)

HOW holy and how beloved, well pleasing and humble, peaceful and sweet and desirable above all to have such a brother who has laid down His life for His sheep.

Letter to All the Faithful

REFLECTION. Of all the amazing things about this knowledge of being welcomed into God's family is the fact that it has already happened. We do not have to wait for it.

And what is yet to come can only be even more amazing!

PRAYER. *Beloved, we are God's children now. What we shall become has not yet been revealed.* (1 Jn 3:2)

INCE He has suffered so many things for us and has done and will do so much good for us, let every creature which is in heaven and on earth and in the sea render praise to God.

Letter to All the Faithful

REFLECTION. As we read holy books, it can be tempting to skip the prayers of praise, or to read over them quickly. It takes a certain mood to really enter into a spirit of praise.

But it's worth the effort to enter into praise. The Bible says this is what we'll be doing for all eternity.

PRAYER. *Day and night they never stop saying, "Holy, holy, holy is the Lord God Almighty."*

(Rev 4:8b)

 ENDER praise to God; for He is our strength and power Who alone is good, alone most high, alone almighty and admirable, glorious and holy, praiseworthy and blessed forever and ever. Amen.

Letter to All the Faithful

REFLECTION. Because the blessed spend eternity praising God, it can't be a trivial thing.

One could spend hours reflecting on each word in Francis' praise. Look at the praises in the Bible and you'll see that they are equally complex. Praise is a powerful form of prayer.

PRAYER. *Worthy is the Lamb that was sacrificed to receive power and riches, wisdom and strength, honor glory and praise.* *(Rev 5:12)*

UT [there are] those who do not do penance and who do not receive the Body and Blood of our Lord Jesus Christ, and give themselves to vices and sins, and walk after evil and bad desires.

NOV. 4

Letter to All the Faithful

REFLECTION. It is not a given that all people will praise God and follow Him. Look around to see how obvious this is!

We must face the fact that there is an alternative to serving God, and that it has consequences.

PRAYER. *Then he will say, "I do not know you or where you come from. Depart from me you evildoers."*
(Lk 13:27)

 HOSE] who do not observe what they have promised, corporally they serve the world, and its fleshly desires and cares and solicitudes for this life.

NOV. 5

Letter to All the Faithful

REFLECTION. In an affluent society like ours, the desires of the body get pretty spoiled and used to being served.

Francis realizes that to serve the flesh is to be led away from God in that our body is also part of our "self" before God.

PRAYER. *Do you not know that your body is a temple of the Holy Spirit within you?* (1 Cor 6:19)

ENTALLY they serve the devil, de- **NOV.**
ceived by him whose sons they are
and whose works they do; blind **6**
they are because they see not the
true light,—our Lord Jesus Christ.

Letter to All the Faithful

REFLECTION. The devil is a liar and a deceiver,
which means that all of his influence goes
through the mind in the form of the lies he tells.

The lies keep us in the dark, unless we follow
Jesus, Who is the light of the world.

PRAYER. *The one who follows me will never
walk in darkness. Rather, he will have the light
of life.* (Jn 8:12)

EWARE, you blind, deceived by the **NOV.**
world, the flesh and by the devil—for it
is sweet to the body to commit sin and **7**
bitter to serve God because all vices and
sins come forth from the heart of man.

Letter to All the Faithful

REFLECTION. Nobody can deny that it is sweet
to commit sin and bitter to serve God, but only
at first. Eventually sin grows bitter, and serving
God grows sweet.

This is why we must persevere in doing
good.

PRAYER. *If we do not give up, we will reap our
harvest in due time.* (Gal 6:9)

YOU think to possess for long the vanities of this world, but you are deceived; for a day and an hour will come of which you think not and do not know and are ignorant of.

NOV.

8

Letter to All the Faithful

REFLECTION. It is important to understand how transitory and short this life is.

Of all the things we become attached to, we should carefully consider what is temporary and what is eternal.

PRAYER. *And the world with all its enticements is passing away, but whoever does the will of God abides forever.*

(1 Jn 2:17)

THE body grows feeble, death approaches, neighbors and friends come saying: "Put your affairs in order." And his wife and his children, neighbors and friends make believe to weep.

NOV.

9

Letter to All the Faithful

REFLECTION. Throughout history, philosophers and wise men have placed a human skull on their desk to remind them of how short their life is.

This is in clear opposition to plastic surgery and all the other things that make up the culture of eternal youth.

PRAYER. *Teach us to comprehend how few our days are so that our hearts may be filled with wisdom.*

(Ps 90:12)

UT let all know that where a man may **NOV.** die in criminal sin, without satisfaction, **10** the devil snatches his soul from his body with such violence and anguish as no one can know except him who suffers it. Letter to All the Faithful

REFLECTION. It is tempting to ignore hell and the possibility of eternal punishment.

But hell and damnation are so clearly and forcefully presented in Scripture and spoken of by Jesus Himself that one must be prepared.

PRAYER. *Depart from me, you accursed, into the eternal fire prepared for the devil and his angels.* (Mt 25:41)

, BROTHER Francis, your little servant, **NOV.** pray and conjure you to receive these **11** words of our Lord Jesus Christ with humility and charity and to put them in practice kindly and to observe them perfectly. Letter to All the Faithful

REFLECTION. Why is it important to receive these words with humility and charity? Perhaps it is because obedience is most often thwarted by pride and lack of love.

The reward of obedience is humility and the reward of humility is peace, as those know who have suffered the pain to get there.

PRAYER. *God opposes the proud, but gives grace to the humble.* (Jas 4:6)

166

N THE Name of the Father and of the Son and of the Holy Ghost. Amen.

Letter to All the Faithful

REFLECTION. Francis ends the letter with the Sign of the Cross. The Sign of the Cross is a central element of our faith, but too often we lose our fervor and it looks like we're swatting flies.

To make the Sign of Cross reverently is to perform a meaningful and powerful act.

PRAYER. *Make disciples of all nations, baptizing them in the name of the Father and of the Son and of the Holy Spirit.* (Mt 28:19)

 O ALL the simple and obedient brothers, the first and the last, Brother Francis, a mean and fallen man, your little servant, gives greeting in Him Who has redeemed and washed us in His Precious Blood.

Letter to All the Friars

REFLECTION. In his old age and illness, Francis wrote a letter to his brothers. He poured out what was most important to him—obedience and reverence for the Blessed Sacrament.

In addition, he makes a frank confession of his sins.

PRAYER. *Confess your sins to one another and pray for one another.* (Jas 5:16)

HEAR, my lords, my sons and my brothers, and with your ears receive my words. Incline the ear of your heart and obey the voice of the Son of God. **NOV. 14**
Letter to All the Friars

REFLECTION. The ear of your heart is an interesting concept, and one found in the rule of St. Benedict where the emphasis is on listening with intelligence and love.

This dual type of listening is imperative to understanding God's word.

PRAYER. *Turn your ears to wisdom and apply your heart to understanding.* *(Prov 2:2)*

PRAISE Him for He is good and extol Him in your works, for therefore He has sent you through all the world that by word and deed you may bear witness to His voice. **NOV. 15**
Letter to All the Friars

REFLECTION. To "bear witness" to something is not a concept we have a lot of experience with in the 21st Century. Perhaps the closest we have are celebrity endorsements, when they assure us, "It works!"

So perhaps we can think of our bearing witness to Christ as being His spokes-man or woman to the world.

PRAYER. *We are ambassadors for Christ, as if God were appealing through us.* *(2 Cor 5:20)*

PERSEVERE under discipline and obedience and with a good and firm purpose fulfil what you have promised Him. The Lord God offers Himself to you as to His sons. NOV. 16 *Letter to All the Friars*

REFLECTION. Persevere with a good and firm purpose. Is this not the perfect summary of a life well lived?

The good and firm purpose we are to focus on is our Christian commitment and all it entails. The reward is nothing less than being part of the family of God!

PRAYER. *Remain faithful to the end, and I will give you the crown of life.* *(Rev 2:10)*

BROTHERS, I entreat you all to show all reverence and all honor possible to the most holy Body and Blood of our Lord Jesus Christ. NOV. 17 *Letter to All the Friars*

REFLECTION. C.S. Lewis once pointed out that the two most holy things that you will encounter in this world are the Eucharist and another human being.

A deep reverence and respect for the Eucharist and for our neighbor should be the standard for all Christians.

PRAYER. *Because there is one bread, we who are many are one body, for we all partake of the one bread.* *(1 Cor 10:17)*

UT let every will, in so far as the grace of the Almighty helps, be directed to Him, desiring to please the High Lord Himself alone. **NOV. 18**
Letter to All the Friars

REFLECTION. It is important to understand the role that our will plays in directing our lives. The will is the force that steers our actions. Our mind may choose the action, but the will carries it out.

Francis urges us to direct all the efforts of our will to pleasing God.

PRAYER. *Sin is crouching at your door. It wants to rule you, but you must overcome it.* *(Gen 4:7)*

 F THE Blessed Virgin Mary is honored because she bore Him in her most holy womb, how holy, just, and worthy ought he to be who touches with his hands, who receives with his heart and his mouth. **NOV. 19**
Letter to All the Friars

REFLECTION. Few of us would feel worthy to step into the shoes of Mary of Nazareth, who bore Jesus inside her and brought Him into the world.

Yet, each time we approach Communion, we are honored to receive Jesus into our own body.

PRAYER. *Whoever eats my flesh and drinks my blood dwells in me and I in him.* *(Jn 6:56)*

T IS a great misery and a deplorable weakness when you have Him thus present to care for anything else in the whole world.

Letter to All the Friars

REFLECTION. It is truly hard to fathom the incredible honor and value of the Eucharist. When we are tempted to sleep in or go to the game rather than go to Mass, it doesn't seem like a big deal.

But to prefer anything to Jesus is to misjudge the gift of the Eucharist.

PRAYER. *The queen of the South came to hear the wisdom of Solomon, but there is one greater than Solomon here.* (Mt 12:42)

 ET the entire man be seized with fear; let the whole world tremble; let heaven exult when Christ, the Son of the Living God, is on the altar in the hands of the priest.

Letter to All the Friars

REFLECTION. The Catholic Mass is one of the few Christian worship services that includes kneeling. In fact, it is probably the only time most Catholics kneel.

This ancient posture of submission is fitting for the awesomeness of the moment.

PRAYER. *Let us bow down and worship him. Let us kneel before the Lord, our Maker.* (Ps 95:6)

HUMBLE sublimity! O sublime humility! That the Lord of the universe, God and the Son of God, so humbles Himself that for our salvation He hides Himself under a morsel of bread. **NOV. 22** Letter to All the Friars

REFLECTION. God does the most amazing things in the most common manner. The newborn baby, the sunset, the touch of a loved one—so miraculous, and yet so commonplace.

It is no surprise, then, that Christ comes to us under the appearance of bread. So miraculous, and so common.

PRAYER. *Do you have eyes and fail to see?*

(Mk 8:18a)

 WARN all my brothers, wherever they may find the divine written words to venerate them so far as they are able, honoring in the words the Lord Who has spoken. **NOV. 23** Letter to All the Friars

REFLECTION. There is an old gospel song called, "Dust on the Bible." It is a striking image that reminds us that the Bible is not just another book.

Francis equates reverence of the Bible with reverence for Christ Himself.

PRAYER. *When I found your words I devoured them. They became a joy to me, the delight of my heart.* *(Jer 15:16)*

MOREOVER I confess all my sins to God the Father and to the Son and to the Holy Ghost and to the Blessed Mary ever Virgin and to all the Saints, and to all the priests of our order and to all my other blessed brothers. *Letter to All the Friars*

REFLECTION. Francis confesses his sins to a rather long list of people!

This long list underscores the fact that sin is not a private thing, and many people are hurt by our sins, beginning with ourselves.

PRAYER. *If we claim that we are sinless, we are only deceiving ourselves, and the truth is not in us.* *(1 Jn 1:8)*

 I HAVE offended in many ways through my grievous fault, by reason of my negligence or weakness or because I am ignorant and simple. *Letter to All the Friars*

REFLECTION. It always seems odd when Saints speak of their sins. Perhaps it is their very purity and nearness to perfection that makes their sins seem all the more serious.

One cast off dirty sock sticks out more in a spotless bedroom than in a messy one.

PRAYER. *Therefore, strive to be perfect, just as your heavenly Father is perfect.* *(Mt 5:48)*

ALMIGHTY, eternal, just, and merciful God, give to us wretches to do for Thee what we know Thee to will and to will always that which is pleasing to Thee. **NOV. 26** Letter to All the Friars

REFLECTION. We spoke earlier of the will as the driver of our conduct. For those who live a Christian life, we strive to will nothing but what God wills. And what God wills is known through His word and His Church.

To make our wills one with God's will is the ultimate goal of all Christians.

PRAYER. *Father, not my will but yours be done.*

(Lk 22:42b)

SO THAT inwardly purified, inwardly illumined and kindled by the flame of the Holy Ghost, we may be able to follow in the footsteps of Thy Son, our Lord Jesus Christ. **NOV. 27** Letter to All the Friars

REFLECTION. Whether we know it or not, we are always influenced and guided by the people in our lives and the things we choose to spend our time with.

The life of Christ is the model and measure of every Christian life.

PRAYER. *Christ himself suffered for you and left an example for you to follow in his footsteps.*

(1 Pet 2:21)

ND by Thy grace alone may we come to Thee the Most High, who in perfect Trinity and simple Unity lives and reigns in the glory of God Almighty forever and ever. Amen.

NOV. **28**

Letter to All the Friars

REFLECTION. The Holy Trinity is the highest, most powerful, most perfect reality that we can ever imagine.

It is right that we should praise and honor the Father, Son, and Holy Spirit with our lives as long as we shall live.

PRAYER. *How good it is to sing praises to our God. How pleasant it is to give him fitting praise.* (Ps 147:1)

N THE subject of thy soul; those things which impede thee in loving the Lord God and whoever may be a hindrance to thee, all these things thou ought to reckon as a favor.

NOV. **29**

To a Certain Minister

REFLECTION. Once when visiting England, a man witnessed a great storm that knocked down many large trees. The overturned trees revealed a very small root structure for such large trees.

The winds were never strong enough in that part of the country to drive the roots deep into the ground.

PRAYER. *It is necessary for us to undergo many hardships in order to enter the Kingdom of God.* (Acts 14:22b)

ND love those that do such things to thee and wish not other from them, save in so far as the Lord may grant to thee; and in this thing love them, —by wishing that they may be better Christians. To a Certain Minister

REFLECTION. Do not wish other than hindrances, challenges, and strife from others.

The secret to such a disposition is that one can always be happy. If challenges come, they are ready and prepared for them. If challenges do not come, it is a pleasant surprise.

PRAYER. *If a righteous man strikes me, I regard it as a kindness.* (Ps 141:5a)

 PLAGUE devoured all oxen and sheep. A man obtained water that had washed the sacred wounds of Francis and if but a drop fell upon the sick animals they recovered.
Bonaventure, *The Life of St. Francis*, 13, 6

REFLECTION. As with so many stories in the life of Francis, there are many biblical parallels: the sacred wounds, the sheep and oxen, the pastor and his flock, the sprinkling of water.

This is the power of the biblical record. These are not just images, but basic elements of God's actions.

PRAYER. *The punishment that brought us peace was on him, and by his wounds we are healed.* (Isa 53:5)

E WAS riding on a poor man's ass, and was obliged to pass the night under the edge of a rock. Francis perceived that this poor man was unable to sleep for bitter cold; he touched him and a great warmth came upon him.

DEC. 2

Bonaventure, *The Life of St. Francis*, 13, 7

REFLECTION. The heat of being filled with the Holy Spirit is something that many of the Saints experienced.

The depiction of Jesus' sacred heart with flames and a crown of thorns expresses beautifully the holy burning of self-denial.

PRAYER. *He will baptize you with the Holy Spirit and with fire.* (Lk 3:16)

 EING unable to walk by reason of the nails protruding from his feet, he caused himself to be borne round cities and villages, emaciated as he was, that he might incite others to bear the Cross of Christ.

DEC. 3

Bonaventure, *The Life of St. Francis*, 14, 1

REFLECTION. People learn so much from our words and actions.

Francis' preaching was powerful during his lifetime, and the witness of how he bore his suffering in later years had that same powerful effect.

PRAYER. *I consider that the sufferings of the present are not worth comparing with the glory that is to be revealed in us.* (Rom 8:8)

E WOULD say: "Let us begin, Brethren, to serve our Lord God, for until now we have made little progress." There is no room for laziness where the spur of love urges us on to greater things.

DEC. 4

Bonaventure, *The Life of St. Francis*, 14, 1

REFLECTION. The constant starting again every day to renew our efforts to serve God is essential to holiness.

Surely holiness requires tremendous energy, both mental and physical.

PRAYER. *The love of Christ urges us on, because we are convinced that one has died for all.* (2 Cor 5:14)

 HAT the merits of the man of God might be increased, merits that find their consummation in endurance, he began to suffer from ailments so grievous that none of his limbs was free from pain and suffering.

DEC. 5

Bonaventure, *The Life of St. Francis*, 14, 2

REFLECTION. Many people tend to sum up Francis' life in words like poverty, or humility, but it seems that suffering was the keynote of his life.

If we learn anything from Francis it should be the clear connection between self-denial and holiness.

PRAYER. *Deny yourselves, take up your cross and follow me.* (Mt 16:24)

A T LENGTH, by prolonged and continuous sickness, he was brought to such a point that his flesh was wasted away. While he was afflicted by such grievous bodily suffering, he would call his pains "sisters."

DEC. 6

Bonaventure, *The Life of St. Francis*, 14, 2

REFLECTION. When we are visited by Sister Hunger or Brother Illness, can we imitate Francis and embrace them as friends?

Francis' method was not to fight them, but to embrace them for love of the God Who allowed them.

PRAYER. *I rejoice in my sufferings for your sake.*
(Col 1:24)

K ISSING the ground, he cried: "I give Thee thanks, O Lord God, for all these my pains, and if it please Thee, add unto them a hundredfold; do not spare the fulfilling of Thy holy will in me."

DEC. 7

Bonaventure, *The Life of St. Francis*, 14, 2

REFLECTION. Perhaps the secret to self-denial and suffering begins with a complete surrender to God's perfect will.

Perhaps our entire life is nothing but a battle between our own will and God's will. Francis "won" that battle by surrendering to God.

PRAYER. *But seek first the kingdom of God and his righteousness, and all these things will be added to you.*
(Mt 6:33)

HEN the day of his departure was at hand, he prostrated himself, lifted his face toward heaven, covered the wound in his side, and said: "I have done what was mine to do, may Christ teach you what is yours."

DEC. 8

Bonaventure, *The Life of St. Francis*, 14, 3

REFLECTION. Everyone who takes the vow as a Franciscan embraces the life that Francis lived, of poverty, suffering, and humility.

But that is not everyone's path. For others, in business or family life, they must learn what is theirs.

PRAYER. *But when the Spirit of truth comes, he will guide you into all the truth.* (Jn 16:13)

E CHARGED the Brethren that when he was dead, to leave him lying naked on the ground for a quarter hour.

DEC. 9

Bonaventure, *The Life of St. Francis*, 14, 4

REFLECTION. Nakedness is a confused concept in our world, evidenced by the efforts we make to conceal, and then to reveal, our body parts.

Perhaps we need to separate the concept of nakedness from nudity to understand the spiritual ramifications of how we dress.

PRAYER. *Naked I came from my mother's womb, and naked I will depart.* (Job 1:21)

S THE hour of his departure was fast approaching he spoke of observing patience, and poverty and fidelity unto the Holy Roman Church, placing the Holy Gospel before all other ordinances.

DEC. 10

Bonaventure, *The Life of St. Francis*, 14, 5

REFLECTION. Patience, poverty, and fidelity to the Catholic Church and the Gospel were the final topics of Francis' teaching.

Because Francis' life was consistent with these themes, he could speak these words with power.

PRAYER. *Love bears all things, believes all things, hopes all things, endures all things.*
(1 Cor 13:7)

 E ADDED: "Be strong, all ye my sons, in the fear of the Lord, and abide in it for ever. And, since temptation and trials will come, blessed are they who shall continue in the works that they have begun."

DEC. 11

Bonaventure, *The Life of St. Francis*,14, 5

REFLECTION. All success in life comes down to perseverance.

At the end of his life, Francis knew that he had persevered, and in his final moments he highlights the importance of not giving up.

PRAYER. *But the one who stands firm to the end will be saved.*
(Mt 24:13)

AT LENGTH, when all the mysteries had been fulfilled in him, and his most holy spirit was freed from the flesh and absorbed into the boundless depths of the divine glory, the blessed man fell asleep in the Lord.

DEC. 12

Bonaventure, *The Life of St. Francis*, 14, 6

REFLECTION. The passing of a Saint always signals a moment of challenge for those who knew and relied on them.

At the same time, we celebrate a Saint's feast day on the day of their death, as if the transition to heaven is the most important moment of a truly full life.

PRAYER. *And the children of Israel wept for Moses in the plains of Moab thirty days.*   (Deut 34:8)

ONE of his Brethren saw that blessed soul, like of a star exceeding bright, mounting in a straight course to heaven; the larks flocked in great numbers to the roof with songs even gladder than usual.

DEC. 13

Bonaventure, *The Life of St. Francis*, 14, 6

REFLECTION. Francis' death was attended by many signs and wonders.

In those moments we see how thin the veil is between heaven and earth.

PRAYER. *Suddenly a chariot of fire and horses of fire appeared and separated the two of them, and Elijah went up to heaven in a whirlwind.*   (2 Ki 2:11)

AT ONCE the holy man began to shine in the glory of many miracles, now that he himself was reigning with Christ... so that belief might be thoroughly confirmed.

DEC.
14

Bonaventure, *The Life of St. Francis*, 15, 6

REFLECTION. To be canonized a Saint, the Catholic Church requires proof that the person is in heaven. This is usually confirmed by miracles.

The intercessory power of the Christian Saint is made greater by their proximity to God.

PRAYER. *The twenty-four elders fell down before the Lamb. . . . they were holding golden bowls full of incense, which are the prayers of God's people.* (Rev 5:8)

EVEN as that blessed man in life had been distinguished by marvelous tokens of virtue, so too from the day of his departure to this present time, he shines throughout the world.

DEC.
15

Bonaventure, *The Life of St. Francis*, 15, 6

REFLECTION. Perhaps the most powerful miracle of St. Francis is the way he continues to inspire us even 500 years after his death.

That is the power of the Saints—the force of their spirit remains in the world leading others to holiness.

PRAYER. *Therefore, encourage one another, and build each other up, as you are all doing.* (1 Thes 5:11)

N HEARING within his soul his Friend's voice of invitation Francis without hesitation arose, and as another Samson strengthened by God's grace, shattered the fetters of a flattering world. **DEC. 16**

Mira Circa Nos, 3, Pope Gregory IX

REFLECTION. In his Papal Bull canonizing St. Francis, Pope Gregory IX used many biblical images to express Francis' life.

The image of Francis with the physical strength of Samson is jarring, but a great allegory for his spiritual power.

PRAYER. *Now when he was come to the place of the Philistines shouting, the spirit of the Lord came strongly upon Samson.* (Jdg 15:14)

 FTER the example of our father Abraham, this man forgot not only his country and acquaintances, but also his father's house, to go to a land which the Lord had shown him by divine inspiration. **DEC. 17**

Mira Circa Nos, 4. Pope Gregory IX

REFLECTION. To leave one's homeland and start over in a new place is difficult.

Trusting in God is the first part of self-denial that leads to holiness, the "tearing down" that leads to being built back up again in Christ.

PRAYER. *The Lord said to Abram, "Leave your country and your people. Leave your father's family and go to the land that I will show you."* (Gen 12:1

E REALLY did not live for himself any longer, but rather for Christ, who died for our sins and rose for our justification, that we might no longer be slaves to sin.

DEC. 18

Mira Circa Nos, 4, Pope Gregory IX

REFLECTION. The one battle we will fight our entire life is the battle with our own self will.

Those who manage to die to self are truly the most successful human beings in this world.

PRAYER. *It is no longer I who live, but Christ who lives in me.*

(Gal 2:20)

 PROOTING his vices and like Jacob arising at the Lord's command he renounced all and took up the battle with the world, the flesh and the spiritual forces of wickedness on high.

DEC. 19

Mira Circa Nos, 4, Pope Gregory IX

REFLECTION. Uprooting one's vices means to enter into a difficult spiritual battle. And the spiritual battle is real.

There are forces which fight against us with temptations and offers of self-indulgence that make it more difficult to overcome our selfish desires.

PRAYER. *Be strong in the Lord and in his great power. Put on God's armor so that you can fight against the devil's clever tricks.*

(Eph 6:10-11)

FTER he had made of his heart an altar for the Lord, he offered upon it the incense of devout prayers to be taken up to the Lord at the hands of angels whose company he would soon join.

DEC. 20

Mira Circa Nos, 4, Pope Gregory IX

REFLECTION. What does it mean to make one's heart an altar for the Lord? An altar is a place to offer sacrifice to God.

Francis' inmost being was the place where he offered his sacrifices to God. There was no pretense in his devotion.

PRAYER. *I beg you therefore, my brethren, by the mercies of God, that you present your bodies as living sacrifices, holy and acceptable to God.* (Rom 12:1)

 S HE had received the sevenfold grace of the Spirit and the help of the eight beatitudes of the Gospel, he journeyed to the house of God.

DEC. 21

Mira Circa Nos, 4, Pope Gregory IX

REFLECTION. The Bible is full of lists: the eight Beatitudes and the ten Commandments, the seven gifts and the nine fruits of the Spirit.

These are like catalogues of God's gifts to us that we should memorize, internalize, and use on our journey to heaven.

PRAYER. *His disciples came to him, and he began to teach them.* (Mt 5:12)

SOWING his seed in tears, he would come back rejoicing carrying his sheaves to the storehouse of eternity.

Mira Circa Nos, 5, Pope Gregory IX

DEC.
22

REFLECTION. The images of the spiritual life being similar to the work of a farm underscore the way God's world works. As with farming, the spiritual life requires a lot of hard work.

The price is always paid up front and in full before you get any benefit from it. The sowing must come before reaping.

PRAYER. *Those who sow in tears will reap in joy.*

(Ps 126:5)

SURELY he sought not his own interests, but those of Christ, serving Him zealously like the proverbial bee.

Mira Circa Nos, 5, Pope Gregory IX

DEC.
23

REFLECTION. Each line of the Papal Bull canonizing St. Francis sums up so well the characteristics that make a Saint.

To renounce what we want and to live zealously for Christ, working at it unfailingly always is at the heart of sanctity.

PRAYER. *All the others serve their own interests more than those of Jesus Christ.* *(Phil 2:21)*

187

HE TOOK in his hands a lamp with which to draw the humble by the example of his glorious deeds, and a trumpet wherewith to recall the shameless with stern and fearsome warnings from their wickedness.

Mira Circa Nos, 5, Pope Gregory IX

REFLECTION. It takes humility to hear the words of the Saint and to be drawn by his or her light.

To the wicked, the powerful holiness of the Saint is like a trumpet that calls them out of their stupor, as we saw with the overwhelming popularity of Mother Teresa and Pope St. John Paul II.

PRAYER. *He shone in his days as the morning star in the midst of a cloud, and as the moon at the full.* (Sir 50:6)

HE CAPTURED the weapons on which the well-armed man trusted while guarding his house and parceling out his spoils, and he led captivity captive in submission to Jesus Christ.

Mira Circa Nos, 5, Pope Gregory IX

REFLECTION. To strive for holiness is a constant battle to overcome ourselves, and then the devil and the forces that work against God.

We do well to focus on the interior battle where we can do the most good, and where we most often lose before we begin.

PRAYER. *Make every effort to supplement your faith with virtue, and virtue with knowledge, and knowledge with self-control.* (2 Pet 1:5-6)

AFTER defeating the threefold earthly enemy, he did violence to the kingdom of heaven and seized it by force. After many glorious battles in this life he triumphed over the world and returned to the Lord.

Mira Circa Nos, 6, Pope Gregory IX

DEC. 26

REFLECTION. Jesus spoke of taking heaven by force. The images of sheep notwithstanding, there is a clear call in the Gospel for us to be forceful and aggressive.

Francis' life was one of constant pushing and shaping the world around him by sheer force of personality and the example of his life.

PRAYER. *The kingdom of heaven suffers violence, and the violent take it by force.* (Mt 11:12)

PLAINLY a life such as his, so holy, so passionate, so brilliant, was enough to win him a place in the Church Triumphant.

Mira Circa Nos, 7, Pope Gregory IX

DEC. 27

REFLECTION. It seems obvious that Francis should be considered as having gained his reward in the heavenly gathering.

While the witness of a holy life is not the only requirement for sainthood, it is the first and most basic element of sainthood.

PRAYER. *Let no one despise you for your youth, but set the believers an example in speech, in conduct, in love, in faith, in purity.* (1 Tim 4:12)

N HIS generosity the omnipotent and merciful declared through many brilliant miracles that his life has been acceptable to God and his memory should be honored by the Church Militant.

DEC.
28

Mira Circa Nos, 7, Pope Gregory IX

REFLECTION. In addition to a life of holiness, the Church requires that the deceased Saint perform miracles through his or her intercession.

Bonaventure's "Life" recounts many such miracles that happened after Francis' death by his intercession.

PRAYER. *There will be great joy in heaven over one sinner who repents.* (Lk 15:7)

 INCE the wondrous events of his glorious life are well known and since we are convinced by reliable witnesses of many brilliant miracles, we decree that he be enrolled in the catalogue of saints worthy of veneration.

DEC.
29

Mira Circa Nos, 8, Pope Gregory IX

REFLECTION. With these words Pope Gregory offered Francis to all the Christian faithful as a patron, role model, and friend in heaven.

There are countless holy men and women in the communion of Saints that we can look to, and call on, and model our lives after.

PRAYER. *Since we are surrounded by so great a cloud of witnesses, let us lay aside every weight of sin which clings to us, and let us run the race that is set before us.* (Heb 12:1)

E DECREE that his birth be cele- **DEC.**
brated worthily and solemnly by
the universal Church on the fourth **30**
of October, the day on which he
entered the kingdom of heaven.

Mira Circa Nos, 9, Pope Gregory IX

REFLECTION. The Church has always been very observant of special dates and anniversaries.

Indeed, the primary calendars of the world have been indelibly shaped by the Judeo-Christian tradition.

PRAYER. *This day is to be a memorial for you, and you are to celebrate it as a festival to the* LORD. . . . *from generation to generation.* (Ex 12:14)

ENCE, we beg, admonish and exhort **DEC.**
all of you to implore his patronage, so
that through his intercession and **31**
merits you might be found worthy of
joining his company with the help of
Him who is blessed forever. Amen.

Mira Circa Nos, 10, Pope Gregory IX

REFLECTION. The canonization of Francis ends with the papal exhortation to seek his intercession and to share in his merits.

Saints constantly call us to join them as Saints in our heavenly homeland.

PRAYER. *To all those in Rome who are loved by God and called to be saints: grace to you and peace from God our Father and the Lord Jesus Christ.* (Rom 1:7)

FROM THE TESTAMENT OF
SAINT FRANCIS

We adore you,
most holy Lord Jesus Christ,
here and in all the churches of the world,
and we bless you, because,
by your holy cross you have redeemed the world.
Amen.

SAINT FRANCIS' PRAYER BEFORE
THE CRUCIFIX

Most High, glorious God,
enlighten the darkness of my heart and give me
true faith, certain hope, and perfect charity,
sense and knowledge, Lord, that l may carry out
your holy and true command. Amen.

SAINT FRANCIS'
VOCATION PRAYER

Most High, Glorious God,
enlighten the darkness of our minds.
Give us a right faith, a firm hope and a perfect charity,
so that we may always and in all things act according
to your holy will. Amen.